A History of
THE WORSHIPFUL COMPANY
OF FARMERS

The Master, HRH The Princess Royal, KG, KT, GCVO

A History of
THE WORSHIPFUL COMPANY
OF FARMERS

THE FIRST FIFTY YEARS 1952-2002

Michael Berlin

Phillimore

Of this Edition 1,000 copies have been printed

This copy is No. 41

2001

Published by
PHILLIMORE & CO. LTD.
Shopwyke Manor Barn, Chichester, West Sussex

ISBN 1 86077 169 6

Printed in Great Britain by
BOOKCRAFT LTD.
Midsomer Norton

CONTENTS

LIST OF ILLUSTRATIONS

Frontispiece: The Master, HRH The Princess Royal, KG, KT, GCVO

Colour Plates

between pages 66 and 67

Acknowledgements to Illustrations

Gerald Sharp, Photographers (Brian Garfield): Plates 2, 24, 40, 41 and 48, Colour
Plates frontispiece; I-IV; Rural History Centre, University of Reading, Plates 4 and
11; Publifoto, Plate 5; Quay Studios, Exeter, Plate 8; Countrywide Photographic,
Plate 9; Christie's Images Ltd., Plates 38 and 39.
     The rest of the illustrations are from the Company's archive.

FOREWORD

by

The Master,
HRH The Princess Royal, KG, KT, GCVO

BUCKINGHAM PALACE

During the 1939/45 World War, the whole of agriculture and its ancillary trades united under the Duke of Gloucester's Red Cross and St John of Jerusalem Appeal Organisation to raise funds for the war effort. This co-operation was so successful that the Committee felt that after the war a united agriculture should continue in some form and, through the efforts of a few dedicated members, a Company was formed with the object of petitioning for a Grant of Livery from the Corporation of London. Eventually, after much effort, a Grant of Livery was approved in 1952. On the occasion of the Company's Jubilee it is therefore appropriate that the history of its growth and achievement should be recorded.

Much has been achieved in the Company's first 50 years and its charitable and educational funds have increased beyond the Founders' wildest dreams. In the new millennium there will be many changes, not only in agriculture, but the Company will move with the times and adapt to meet the challenge. As the first Lady Liveryman of the Company and subsequently as a member of the Court serving as Junior Warden, Senior Warden and now its Master, I am able to appreciate the great service given by many members of the Livery. We owe a debt to them and to the Founders of the Company.

Anne

PREFACE

The Livery Companies of London, of which the Worshipful Company of Farmers stands eightieth in precedence, are ancient institutions which since the early middle ages have played a vital part in the history of the City of London. Originally founded as trade guilds, they regulated the crafts and professions of the City and took part in the running of civic government through regular assemblies at the Guildhall as well as at their own livery halls. They drew inspiration from the religious confraternities that met regularly on the anniversaries of various patron saints at London's parish churches in acts of collective worship and conviviality. As the term suggests, the London companies were bodies of men following a particular occupation incorporated by charters and letters patent and entitled to wear their distinctive livery gowns at ceremonial events, such as the annual election of the City's Lord Mayor. The customary prefix 'Worshipful' denoted the privileged status of the livery companies in regulating the social and economic life of the City. Freedom of the City of London was a requisite for membership of the livery companies and up to 1835 the only method of obtaining freedom of the City was through membership of the livery companies. Only Freemen of the livery companies were allowed to do business and vote in civic elections. Voting in elections of the Sheriff and Lord Mayor was restricted to liverymen. Admission to the freedom of the City and the livery was obtained in one of three ways: servitude, patrimony and redemption. Servitude entailed a period as an apprentice undergoing training and service for up to seven years. Patrimony was the right of membership based on the membership of the father, if the child was born after the father became a liveryman. Freedom by redemption was through payment of a fee at the discretion of the governors of the guilds.

The guilds were also important administrators of charitable bequests involving the welfare and education of those engaged in the trades and crafts associated with each guild. Over the centuries, as the City's population expanded, the guilds were augmented with new trades and industries. New livery companies were founded in the 17th century but thereafter no new livery companies were established until the 20th century. The Worshipful Company of Farmers, founded in the years after the Second World War, is one of the new foundations of the modern era. Since the medieval period the livery companies have changed as institutions: they have lost their role as regulators of trade but have remained as part of the civic government of the City of London and as administrators of diverse forms of charity in the form of schools, almshouses and other gifts. Today the livery companies continue this ethos of charity, conviviality and good works. The Farmers are a part of this evolving tradition.

The foundation of the Worshipful Company of Farmers and its subsequent history took place against a backdrop of dramatic and fundamental transformation of British agriculture. Emerging out of a severe depression during the inter-war period, when many thousands of family farms floundered, Britain's farms were revolutionised by the demands of wartime and the immediate post-war years. This period was marked by a concerted drive for increased productivity through mechanisation and the application of scientific methods to agriculture. The role of the state in the guaranteeing of a market for farmers' products came together in the Agriculture Act of 1947 which became the benchmark by which post-war governments dealt with the agricultural sector. The net result of these changes was a massive boost to productivity and a sea change in the ways in which food was grown. Farming came to be seen more and more as an industry in its own right and the methods and customs of modern industry—management and mechanisation, modern marketing—began to figure amongst the farmer's concerns. The entry of the United Kingdom into the European Economic Community in January 1973 marked a further watershed for Britain's farmers. The controversial impact of the Common Agricultural Policy (CAP) heightened the sense in which Britain's farmers were part of a much wider system of food production and marketing—a multi-million pound industry. If the traditions of guild membership are rooted in the past, the origins of the Farmers' Company occurred in an entirely modern context.

AUTHOR'S NOTE AND ACKNOWLEDGEMENTS

As the Company celebrates its Jubilee in 2002 in the same year as Her Majesty celebrates her Jubilee, the Court of Assistants felt that the occasion should be marked by authorising the production of this history to enable the Livery and the public to appreciate how the Worshipful Company of Farmers came to be founded and its achievement to date.

The author wishes to thank Past Masters Ronald Borner, Michael Foreman and Trevor Kemsley for their direction and advice in the composition of this history. Their untiring and attentive support has greatly contributed to the success of this project. Thanks are also due to Past Masters Arnold Hitchcock, Derek Pearce, John Borner, Richard Brooks and also Honorary Liveryman Ian Reid for their help with particular aspects of the Company's history. At the Company's request footnotes have been omitted. The main sources for what follows are the Court Minutes and Committee papers of the Worshipful Company of Farmers and the minutes of the General Purposes Committee of the Court of Aldermen and the papers of the Chamberlain and Deputy Keeper of Records of the Corporation of London. Readers wishing to research the Company's history further are advised to consult the Company's archives which are due to be placed on deposit at Guildhall Library.

List of Subscribers

The Master: H.R.H. The Princess Royal
The Lord Mayor of London, 2001/02

R.J.S. Addison
A. Henry Ashby
Mrs. B. Leslie Barker
Thomas Shepherd Bennett
Robert J. Black
R.R.C. Bloomfield
Catherine Borner
John Borner
Ronald Borner
Amy E.A. Brooks
George W.A. Brooks
Richard A. Brooks
John A. Brooks
Dick Broughton
Mr. Grant Buck
Christopher Butler
Sir Richard Butler
Tim Calcutt
Rosie Carne
Mrs. Michael Cheveley
Fenella Copas
Sarah Copas
Tom Arthur Copas
Daniel C. Cornish
John H. Cossins
Jeremy D. Courtney
W. Richard T. Crane
Richard H. Davies
Professor Barry Dent
Rob den Engelse
Alan Evans Hendrick
N.J. Fiske
Mr. Keith M. Flemington
C.J. Foreman
M.C. Foreman
J. Barclay Forrest
Douglas Fox
P.H. Gibbons
Mrs. Herbert Graves
Peter and Henrietta Greig
David Gurney
L.H. Hargreaves
Bob Harrison
Michael H. Hinton
Arnold Q. Hitchcock
Margôt E. Telford Holroyd
Graham A. Jackman
George Jessel
Andrew John
Keith H. Johnson

J.C.R. and J.M. Jones
Richard W. Kemsley
Trevor W. Kemsley
Kerr Kirkwood
Nicholas Lane
Nicholas A. Lane
Lord Lonsdale
Eric W.T. Malcolm
David Margesson
Robert S. Markillie
Alistair J. Marshall
Brian Montgomery
John H.C. Nicholson
C.P.W. Bundgaard Nielsen
Jon Parker
Denis Parton
Derek George Pearce
Vagn Ingemann Pertl
Christopher Pertwee
The Lord Plumb
R.J. Posnett
Creighton T. Redman
Ian G. Reid
Colin D.F. Roberts
Anne Roberts
E.A. Robertson
Julian A. Sayers
Niels Erik Schultz-Petersen
John Service
Anthony Campbell Seymour
Walter Simon
Graham Smith
John South (Beadle)
Robert Steven
John G. Stevens
John M. Stevenson
Ian Arthur Stockley
Andrew Streeter
Simon F.B. Taylor
John Thorne
Trevor Trigg
Merlin Usher-Smith
Allan Wilkinson
Sir Graham Wilkinson, Bt
Vaughan Willshaw
C.J.H. Wilson
John J.H. Wilson
Margaret L. Winter (Clerk)
Barney Wise
Richard A. Woof

Chapter One

THE ORIGINS OF A
MODERN LIVERY COMPANY

An ancient antecedent: the medieval cornmongers' guild

Agriculture can be said to be England's oldest and most important industry though farming was never included as an urban occupation. The well-known urban fable about the Freemen of London having the right to drive sheep across London Bridge is probably apocryphal. Yet the Company can claim a distant predecessor in the City's history. For centuries during the middle ages the growth of London was dependent on the supply of food. Guilds traded in different foodstuffs, their members controlling the markets on the river Thames at Queenhithe and Billingsgate. A guild of Cornmongers was established in London during the 14th century, representing one of the City's most important sources of wealth, the grain trade. London was unique among English towns and cities in that it was the only one to have a specific guild related to the grain trade. The City records for this period contain enigmatic references to what proved to be an ephemeral organisation. The men who controlled this trade, cornmongers or *bladarii* or *blatiers*, were numbered among the City's most wealthy and prominent persons in some lists of citizens, several rising to the offices of Sheriff and Alderman.* In 1316 and 1320 cornmongers represented the City in Parliament. The number of cornmongers grew with the expansion of the population of the City up to the beginning of the 15th century but from 1400 the guild faded away, affected in part by the shrinkage in the size of the grain trade after the population decline caused by the onset of the great outbreak of bubonic plague, the 'Black Death', in 1348. Thereafter the supply of grain fell under the dominance of members of other guilds. The marketing and supply of agricultural produce was in the hands of guilds of fishmongers, brewers, bakers, butchers and fruiterers. The link between

---

* *Bladarii* may be alternatively translated as corn dealer, corn monger or corn chandler. Thus the medieval guild was described as a guild of corn chandlers in a pamphlet issued by the Company in 1954.

agriculture and the City guild tradition was lost until the 20th century when it was revivified in conditions very different from the period of foundation of the medieval guilds. In the 20th century the Company's founders looked back to these ancient antecedents.

Wartime agriculture; 'Comradeship and Team Spirit'

The genesis of the Worshipful Company of Farmers took place amid the tremendous outpouring of voluntary effort shown by the agricultural community during the Second World War. In an age of total war agriculture was a key component of the war effort. It may be difficult for a modern reader, without personal experience of the 1940s, to appreciate the extent to which Britain's fortunes during the war rested on a knife-edge. In the Atlantic Hitler's U-boat fleet had mounted a deadly blockade of Britain's ports, choking off vital supplies of food and material, repeating a strategy which had brought Britain to the brink of starvation during the Great War. From the outbreak of war in 1939 Britain's farms had been under government direction as thousands of acres of pasture and grassland were brought under the plough. The war brought County War Agriculture Executive Committees, Land Army Girls, and the mechanisation of farming on a scale hitherto unseen. In contrast to the tough times of the inter-war years agricultural productivity soared. In both town and countryside the war witnessed an unprecedented display of voluntary work, directed through organisations such as the British Red Cross and the Order of St John of Jerusalem. Volunteers manned the mobile canteens, mounted fire watches, drove ambulances and collected money, scrap metal and other goods for everything from the sponsoring of Spitfires for the R.A.F. to the provision of food parcels for prisoners-of-war. It was from such heroic but entirely humble efforts of ordinary people that the Farmers' Company could trace its beginnings.

The Red Cross Agricultural Fund

A special War Organisation of the British Red Cross was set up under the patronage of the Duke of Gloucester to organise fund raising for its activities at home and overseas. Under the aegis of the Duke of Gloucester's Red Cross and St John Fund, sub-committees were established to cover fund-raising in different fields and among different groups in British society, including the churches, schools, sports and women's organisations. Altogether groups associated with the Red Cross Appeal raised some £57 million through combined voluntary efforts. Agriculture was one of the groups represented. A committee to organise an appeal to the agricultural community on behalf of the Lord Mayor's Appeal for the Duke of Gloucester's Red Cross and St John Fund began its deliberations at the Mansion House on 1 November 1939 under the chairmanship of Sir Charles Howell Thomas. The membership of the Committee, later presided over by the Duke of Norfolk, provided the men who would go on to found the Farmers' Company: Richard Haddon (knighted 1951), who succeeded Sir Charles Howell Thomas as Chairman in 1942, Captain Sir Cleveland Fyfe, Theodore Stephens, Nevill Matthews, and Malcolm Messer. All would go on to serve in the first Court of the Farmers' Company. Alec Dodds Robertson acted as the Agricultural Fund's able and active secretary from 1939 until 1946.* In May 1940 the Agricultural Committee made a public appeal to rural landowners, farmers, land workers and all those associated with agriculture and the land for their co-operation. By the end of February 1941 a nation-wide network of county committees had been established, the secretaries of each county committee being the county secretary of the National Farmers Union with sub-committees set up to cover specialist branches of agriculture. By the end of the war some 18,000 local committees had been formed throughout England and Wales. A special feature of the Fund was the use of a wide variety of ingenious means of raising money. Gift sales, involving the auctioning of prize livestock, the auctioneers providing their services free of charge, raised over £3 million. More than one member of the present-day Farmers' Company can recall from childhood prize calves marked with red crosses being put up often more than once for resale at weekly auctions. It is worth placing on record the remarkable tale of Lt. Colonel Attfield Brooks who later became a Master of the Farmers' Company. Attfield Brooks, while a prisoner-of-war in 1944, wrote to his wife and requested that she auction off a 30-year-old bottle of Irish whiskey at a Red Cross sale at Colchester market in gratitude for the generosity of the Red Cross in sending food parcels to P.O.W.s. The bottle was made Lot 1 and, after being auctioned several times, raised £115 (equal to a present-day value of £9,200). He later commented that but for the Red Cross parcels he would not have survived.

In addition to such sterling efforts a 'Rural Pennies' scheme, based on the nation-wide 'Penny-a-Week Fund' run by the Duke of Gloucester's Appeal, brought in some £2.5 million through local collections by 85,000 village collectors, using whist drives, dances and 'Victory Garden' fêtes to garner support. Virtually every conceivable organisation associated with agriculture took part, including livestock auctioneers, land agents, feed merchants, the Young Farmers and the National Union of Agricultural Workers. Special committees were formed around appeals to beekeepers, owners of racing pigeons and caged bird fanciers. Never before had one umbrella organisation brought together such disparate countryside interests: in all some 40

---

* For his services to the Fund he was made an honorary Liveryman of the Company in 1952.

different organisations took part. As a permanent memorial to the good works carried out, when the Fund reached the figure of £5 million, five red oaks were planted in Windsor Great Park by King George VI, the Queen, Princess Elizabeth and Princess Margaret and the Duke of Norfolk. When the fund closed in 1946 the King ordered the planting of four more trees, the whole forming a cross. A plaque is displayed bearing the following lines selected by the King:

> Through God's good grace,
> through strength of English Oak
> We have preserved our faith, our
> throne, our land;
> Now with our freedom saved from
> tyrant's yoke
> We plant these trees. Remember
> why they stand*

1   Red Cross Agriculture Fund trees in Windsor Great Park (see illustration 53).

---

* In 1974 the Court of Assistants paid a visit of inspection to the Red Cross Oak Trees and, when in 1993 some uncertainty arose about the exact species of the trees, the Deputy Ranger of the Crown Estate at Windsor officially confirmed that there was an obvious anomaly in the wording of the plaque as the oaks were North American red oaks, and that the reference to English Oak was, in the Deputy Ranger's words, 'a way of alluding to English Courage and spirit synonymous with an English Oak'.

The efforts of the Agricultural Fund speak for themselves. Some £8.5 million was raised by the time the Fund was wound up in 1946. It was only natural that those involved would hope to perpetuate this impressive display of wartime solidarity.

On a livery outing to Windsor Great Park and the Castle in May 2000 The Master replaced the one oak that had not survived (see p.100).

From as early as 1940 members of the Committee of the Agricultural Fund were looking ahead to the post-war years and holding informal discussions about how the Fund's good intentions might be perpetuated in time of peace. The Fund's Chairman from 1942, Richard Haddon, used the auspices of the Fund's weekly informal luncheons, held at the Café Royal, as a sounding board for discussing the prospects for keeping alive the spirit of wartime co-operation in the years to come. According to his brief resumé of the Company's early history, written in 1949, 'but for the comradeship and team spirit so manifest at these meetings—Dutch lunches—the Farmers' Company would not have come into being'. At these meetings various ideas for the post-war period were put forward. One, for an 'Association of Agriculture', was eventually launched in 1947 to promote greater public awareness of the national importance of agriculture.[*] Another idea put forward was a scheme for training in agriculture for ex-servicemen through the County Agricultural Committees, Farm Institutes and Colleges. This plan was dropped after it was learned that the Ministry of Agriculture and Fisheries and the Ministry of Education had intentions to set up similar schemes.

'The Company of Agriculturists'

The Chairman's Committee then turned its attention to a proposal put forward by Sir Cleveland Fyfe to form a livery company. The founders could look to other examples of new livery companies. In the recent past two other ancient professions, the Master Mariners and the City of London Solicitors had formed livery companies. The Committee took advice on the subject from a sympathetic Past Master of the Carmen's Company, Victor Parker. Mr. Parker arranged for meetings with the Clerk of the Carmen's Company, Oliver Gordon Sunderland, and the Deputy Keeper of Records of the City of London, Mr. P.E. Jones. Mr. Jones provided the expert advice on how best to go about setting up a livery company and discussed with Sir Cleveland Fyfe the draft ordinances of the new organisation as well as a petition to the Corporation of London requesting recognition as a City livery company. On

---

[*] It is perhaps significant that a large number of the first members of the Council of the Association of Agriculture, including Richard Haddon, Theo F. Stephens, Sir Patrick Gower and the Earl de La Warr, President of the Association, were early members of the Farmers' Company.

23 September 1946 the Chairman's Committee took the momentous decision to establish formally 'The Company of Agriculturists'. The key members of the Agricultural Fund Chairman's Committee were elected as a provisional Court of Assistants, with Richard Haddon and Victor Parker as Senior and Junior Wardens and Sir Cleveland Fyfe as temporary Clerk. Though it is invidious to single out individuals, the moving figures in the foundation of the Company were Richard Haddon and Sir Cleveland Fyfe. Both men had extensive links with both the countryside and the City. Richard Haddon farmed near Windsor but was also managing editor of the London-based trade newspaper *The Farmer and Stock Breeder* * in addition to having acted ably as the Chairman of the Agricultural Fund. Sir Cleveland Fyfe had a long career in agriculture as Parliamentary Secretary and later as Joint General Secretary of the National Farmers Union. His skills were as much those of the town-based journalist and publicist as a man of the soil. He was a Fellow of the Guild of Agricultural Journalists, sat on the Milk Marketing Board and had advised the wartime Ministry of Agriculture on publicity. With such talents it could be expected that the Farmers' Company would easily take its place amongst the older, established livery companies.

---

* Taken over by *Farmers' Weekly*.

Chapter Two

THE ESTABLISHMENT OF THE COMPANY

The Grant of a Livery and Royal Charter 1947-1955

Though the 'Company of Agriculturists' was thus established on paper it could have no official existence until it was duly recognised by the Court of Aldermen of the City of London by means of a Grant of Livery. Without a Grant of Livery the Company could have no formal standing in the City, its members could take no part in civic elections nor could they serve in civic office. Such grants were only acceded to in response to a petition and after much behind-the-scenes lobbying. To this end the Company set about sounding out potential allies within the City. A friend and benefactor of the Company in its early days was Alderman Bracewell Smith (knighted 1946), a member of the Carmen's Company and Chairman of the board of the Café Royal. Prior to the foundation of the Company it was he who had helped the Agricultural Fund Committee to find a suitable room for its 'Dutch lunches', at a time when places for meetings of this sort in London were very difficult to find. The Café Royal was for many years the Company's first 'home'. In recognition of his good services the Committee presented him with a replica of the Florence Nightingale lamp during one of its lunches in early 1946. During the function Richard Haddon and other members of the Committee told Sir Bracewell Smith of their plans for forming a livery company. So it was that when he was elected Lord Mayor later that year the Court of the newly formed Company turned to the new incumbent in hope that the Grant of Livery would speedily be made.

This hope was to prove profoundly over optimistic. Alderman Sir Bracewell Smith informed the Company in early January 1947 that the Court of Aldermen 'were not very anxious to increase the number of livery companies unless those applying have some special activity in the City' and asked the Company to provide some evidence of how long its constitution had been in existence, and of its links with agriculture and more particularly with the City. Research into the City archives about the earlier existence of the Cornmongers' guild was used to buttress claims for a Grant of Livery. Richard Haddon replied to the Lord Mayor's request with a letter detailing the history of the Red Cross Agricultural Fund, the earlier existence of a

Cornmongers' guild and the reasons behind the foundation of the Company. His letter is revealing in that it demonstrates why the members of original Red Cross Agricultural Fund would have wished to perpetuate their organisation as a modern City livery company:

> We had in mind the fact that the Corn and Agricultural Merchants, the Agricultural Engineers, the Seed Trade, the Cattle Food Trade, the Fertiliser Manufacturers, and many other markets, firms and other interests have their national headquarters in the City and that the Farmers' Union, the auctioneers and estate agents and other similar national bodies are housed just outside the City boundaries. It seemed to us, accordingly, that it would be entirely fitting if a Livery Company could be established to represent all branches of the nation's greatest industry and submission of our Petition was agreed for that purpose at the end of last year.

At the same time that it was marshalling these arguments the Company sought to better establish its corporate identity. In deference to opinion in the City its formal title was altered. In March 1947 Richard Haddon wrote to the Lord Mayor to inform him that 'a number of our friends in the City, who wholeheartedly favour the project, have suggested to me that it would be wiser to adopt the title "The Farmers' Company" rather than go forward with the present cumbersome name. They take the view that the simpler style would be far more acceptable to the Court of Aldermen'. The Company's own Court of Assistants saw the advantage to this change and voted unanimously to accept the new designation from March 1947. The Company felt confident enough of its permanent existence to seek the right to display a heraldic coat of arms. The Company approached Lancaster Herald who produced a sketch of the proposed coat of arms. After extensive consultation, during which various

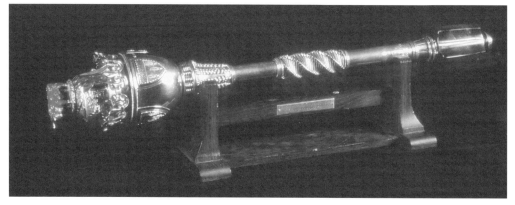

2   The Company's Mace, the gift of the Master, Lord Courthope, M.C., T.D., D.L., and stand made from bog oak from the Ely Fens, the gift of Sir Richard Haddon, C.B.E. (see p. 42).

changes were suggested, a petition for a Grant of Arms was submitted to the Duke of Norfolk, Earl Marshal and Hereditary Marshal of England. Richard Haddon provided photographs of agricultural workers whose dress would serve as a model for the Company's supporters. A celestial bull, also modelled on photographs provided by him, replaced the relatively rare corncrake, which had been originally included, as the Company's crest. The Company's motto, 'Give Us Our Daily Bread' connoted the reliance of farmer on the force of divine providence. The Grant of Arms was bestowed on the Company in March 1948.

At this stage the Company began to look for a suitable candidate for the post of Master. The Company sounded out the Duke of Norfolk, who had served as President of the Agricultural Fund and as Under Secretary at the Ministry of Agriculture during the wartime coalition government. As a member of one of England's most venerable landed families the Duke of Norfolk was a natural choice for this role. The Duke declined this offer with 'profound regret' because of commitments to serve on the Court of the Worshipful Company of Ironmongers. The choice of the Company then fell on Lord Courthope. George Loyd Courthope had a long and illustrious career in agriculture. Born in 1877 of an ancient Sussex landed family, he entered Parliament as Conservative M.P. for the Rye division in 1906 at the tender age of 29, only retiring from the House of Commons in 1945. In 1909 he was Chairman of the Central Chamber of Agriculture. After seeing active service early on in the Great War, in which he was mentioned in despatches, awarded the Military Cross and wounded, he became Assistant Controller of Timber Supplies. After the war he continued his work in forestry. He held, among a string of posts, the offices of President of the British Forestry Association, President of the Central Landowners' Association (which in 1967 was renamed the Country Landowners Association),* Forestry Commissioner, Chairman of the Empire Forestry Association, President of the Royal Agricultural Society, as well as Past Prime Warden of the Goldsmiths' Company. A man of such a wide range of achievements was an obvious candidate after the Duke of Norfolk. As Richard Haddon's historical resumé put it in ringing tones, Lord Courthope was 'a man whom agriculture held in the utmost esteem, a man who put agriculture before party; in fact a man of the soil, respected by everyone connected in farming'. Richard Haddon's history noted how their first Master was to prove an 'essential link between the Country's largest industry and the City of London'. Lord Courthope took office as Master at a Court meeting at the Café Royal on 23 June 1947. He was to continue in that office for the first critical seven years of the Company's existence.

---

*   In 2001 renamed Country Land and Business Association.

From this point the Court of the Company began to meet formally. The early activities of the Company were guided by a General Purposes Committee, which reported regularly to the Court of Assistants. At its first meeting the Court agreed to adopt a draft of its ordinances drawn up by the Clerk of the Carmen's Company, Oliver Gordon Sunderland, who took over from Sir Cleveland Fyfe as Clerk of the Farmers' Company and served with distinction in this office until 1966. The ordinances drawn up by Mr. Gordon Sunderland consisted of 12 clauses detailing the election and duties of officers, the admission of freemen, and other matters such as the auditing of accounts, and payment of quarterage dues, fines and fees. The Company's internal constitution followed the form of the older more established livery companies. It was to be governed by a Court consisting of a Master, a Senior and a Junior Warden and between 20 and 24 Assistants elected by the Company from amongst its own members. In framing the ordinances the Court demonstrated the concerns that had animated the original Café Royal meetings. The most important clauses were its statement of objects which formally committed it to work for the betterment of agriculture, especially with regard to education: 'to encourage and foster agriculture and ancillary occupations in the United Kingdom, by conference and co-operation to bring about maximum production and by scholarships and all other means to promote research and generally foster good husbandry.' Importantly another clause promised to assist any proceedings designed to support these ends and 'to oppose any act, proposal or other matter likely to harm the said occupations'. Though the Company was to remain strictly a non-political organisation it was to act as a quiet champion of the countryside in the fastness of the City of London.

The efforts of the Company to establish itself were thus at this stage successful. An early proposal that would have effectively dissolved the infant organisation was readily seen off. In July 1947 the suggestion that the Company amalgamate itself with the venerable and much older Worshipful Company of Gardeners, which dated from the early 17th century, was politely declined, pending the outcome of the Farmers' petition for its Livery. The Company set about building up membership. Members of the Court were asked to compile lists of potential liverymen. Approaches were made to a wide variety of individuals in farming and related professions such as members of the Royal Agricultural Society of England, veterinary surgeons, surveyors, land agents, livestock auctioneers and agricultural valuers. Among the names submitted were some of the leading lights of post-war British farming. Sir Reginald Dorman Smith, Minister of Agriculture at the time of the foundation of the Red Cross Agricultural Fund, joined in 1947. Tom Williams, M.P. (ennobled 1961), the popular Durham miner who had served in the wartime coalition and as Minister of Agriculture in the Attlee government as well Anthony Hurd, M.P. (ennobled 1964), Chairman of the Conservative back-bench Agriculture Committee, were approached.

Not all those proposed became members. A proposal that Lord Beaverbrook be invited to join was dropped on the grounds that, if he was asked, it would be necessary to issue invitations to join to 'all the other newspaper proprietors in the country'. King George VI was invited to join early on and though he declined on grounds of protocol, he conveyed a message through a letter from Sir Ulick Alexander, the Keeper of the Privy Purse, that 'he is much interested to hear of this new institution, and desires me to convey to you a message of encouragement and good wishes for its success'. As events were to demonstrate, The King's interest was more than mere politeness. The Company could look with satisfaction on the growing size of its membership. By March 1948 membership stood at ninety-four. Within less than a year the number had more than doubled and the Clerk could report confidently that of this 118 members were 'practical farmers' while a further 23 had close connections with the farming industry. By September the following year the Company had grown to 221 members.

The original corps of men who animated the Company in the late 1940s and 1950s contained some powerful individuals with an impressive array of credentials. Crucial figures in the early years of the Company included some of the leading names from the world of farming. William Cumber, a tenant farmer from a long established Berkshire family, was Chairman of the Standing Committee of the Council of Agriculture, President of the British Shire Horse Society and Chairman of the Farmers' Club through the Second World War. Nevill Matthews, who was a very important figure in the running of the Company in the 1950s and early 1960s, was one of Britain's foremost pedigree livestock auctioneers. Stephen Cheveley, a Yorkshireman of Irish extraction, who was one of the moving spirits behind the Company's involvement with Wye College, University of London, had been both a working farmer and head of the agricultural division of Imperial Chemicals Industries, as well as a scientific advisor to the Ministry of Agriculture's Technical Development Committee and to the Foot and Mouth Research Institute. He was also the founder of Plant Protection Ltd. (later a subsidiary of I. C. I.) and an independent consultant. Alderman Sir Ralph Perring, who joined the Company in 1952 and who combined a family furniture business with running a successful dairy and pig farm, proved to be an invaluable friend of the Company in its early years. A member of the Tin Plate Workers' Company, he was raised to the Office of Lord Mayor in 1962. In 1965 he presented a petition to increase the maximum number of the Farmers' Livery to 300 liverymen. The Company received valuable financial advice in its early days from Lord Swaythling, Director of Messrs. Samuel Montagu & Company, the merchant bankers, who farmed on his own account and was involved with the Royal Association of British Dairy Farmers, the Cattle Breeders Association and the Royal Agricultural Society of England. Other important founder members included J.K. Knowles,

General Secretary of the N.F.U., Malcolm Messer, editor of *Farmers' Weekly*, Thomas Neame (knighted in 1961), an East Kent hop farmer and veteran of Gallipolli who was Trustee of the Royal Agricultural Society of England and Chairman of the East Malling Research Station and a Governor of Wye College, Frederick Clare Hawkes, Secretary of the Chartered Auctioneers and Estate Agents' Institute and later President of the College of Estate Management, and Sir Patrick Gower, Chairman and later President of Charles Higham Ltd, an advertising firm specialising in farm accounts, who had had an impressive career as a civil servant, being Private Secretary to no less than three Prime Ministers, Bonar Law, Ramsay Macdonald and Stanley Baldwin.

Despite such an impressive collection of members, formal recognition by the City of London eluded the Farmers. The Company had reasons to be hopeful. As early as July 1947 the Court heard of the 'favourable attitude' of the Court of Aldermen to the petition for a livery and that 'if the petitioners would organise and show useful work for the agricultural community they would favourably consider a grant at a later date'. To this end the Company set about looking into the possibility of setting up travelling bursaries for post-graduates in agricultural studies as well as direct funding of undergraduate scholarships in agriculture. In May 1948 the Master, Lord Courthope, informed the Court that Sir Percy Greenaway, Senior Alderman and Lord Mayor 1932-3, had at a recent City function told him that 'an early presentation of a petition would be favourably received'. Over the next few years Sir Percy may have come to regret expressing this optimistic assessment. The Company jumped with alacrity at the chance of gaining a Grant of Livery. The Court agreed to present a petition to the Court of Aldermen for a Grant of Livery 'at the earliest opportunity'. For the next four years the Company fought hard to obtain recognition from the Court of Aldermen as the formal presentation to the Court of Aldermen of the Company's petition for a Grant of Livery was privately discouraged by the Company's friends on the Aldermanic bench as it was likely to be opposed. In November 1948 the Company was told, via the Town Clerk, that the Court of Aldermen wished presentation of the Company's petition to be deferred until the next year.

In the meantime the Company pressed ahead with plans for an inaugural dinner, which was held, through the good offices of the Master, Lord Courthope, at Goldsmiths' Hall on 9 December 1948. The Lord Mayor and the Bishop of London, among other luminaries, attended. Musical entertainment was provided by an orchestra 'under the leadership of Mr. Ham Hudson' who played 'the latest selection from their repertoire' as well as songs presented by Miss Phyllis Adrian, soprano, and Mr. Gillie Potter 'The B.B.C.'s Gift to the Nation' under the direction of Mr. Victor Marmont. After the no doubt convivial occasion the Company's hopes must have risen when it received the next day a letter of thanks from the Lord Mayor which wished them success 'in a quick march to the livery because I feel quite certain that you will be a most valuable addition to the guildry'. But it was to be more 'long haul' than 'quick march'. In spring 1949 the Clerk sought the advice of Sir George Wilkinson, Stationer and Lord Mayor during the Blitz. Sir George strongly advised the Company to wait a little in proceeding with its petition and the Court duly resolved not to make any further moves until it received his advice. Sir George Wilkinson's help was to prove vital and in recognition of his services to the Company he was clothed as an honorary Liveryman in December 1957.

Aims and Objects: 'A Common Meeting Ground'

The delays encountered by the Company stiffened its resolve to commence with plans for implementing its aims and objects. In June 1948 it entered into informal discussions with Sir Donald Vanderpeer, Permanent Secretary to the Ministry of Agriculture, about the possibility of sponsoring young farmers on overseas visits to the United States and Commonwealth countries. Such exchanges were thought to have an important role in fostering mutual understanding between British, Commonwealth and American agriculture in the post-war period. In September 1949 after lengthy discussion it was resolved that one of the principal aims of the Company should be 'to promote interchange of agricultural students within the British Commonwealth by the award of scholarships and to collaborate for that purpose with any organisation in the United Kingdom, or in the overseas dominions concerned with the advancement of agricultural education'. It was also decided that any action in furtherance of these aims was to be left in abeyance until the Company had received its Grant of Livery.

By early 1950 the Company had still not been given the go-ahead to present its petition. A yet more definitive statement of the Company's aims and objects was formulated by the Company in preparation for the presentation of its petition to the Court of Aldermen. The Senior Warden, Richard Haddon, drafted a covering letter for presentation to the City Corporation. In it he expressed the aims and objects of the Company under five headings: stimulating the development of agricultural education, financial assistance for overseas visits by agricultural students, the maintenance and revival of rural crafts such as thatching, ditching and hedging, the provision of a 'common meeting ground' for farmers and allied professions and finally the promotion of a better understanding of the importance of farming in the economic life of the nation and the close association of farming with the City of London. His letter ended with a look back to the work of the Red Cross Agricultural Fund: 'our programme is ambitious, but our war-time experience had taught us what men of goodwill, banded together for a common purpose, can achieve'.

Despite such ringing sentiments the Company's petition was still stalled. Disappointment was expressed at the Court meeting held in June that the petition had not been presented. The Court was told that, though the Company's sponsor on the Aldermanic bench, Sir Percy Greenaway, was in possession of the document, he had not yet presented it as he was hoping to obtain unanimity for its approval. By mid-September the Court had yet to receive a favourable reply and it was decided that 'they would prefer the petition to be presented forthwith even if it met with opposition in certain quarters'.

The Company went ahead with the presentation of the petition in February 1951 but the Court of Aldermen opted to refer it to the General Purposes Committee and to await a series of reports into the Company by the Chamberlain, the City Solicitor, the Controller and the Deputy Keeper of Records. The deliberations of these important civic officials, whose reports to the General Purposes Committee are deposited in the archives of the Corporation of London, in part perhaps help to explain the degree of opposition to granting official recognition to the Company's petition for a Livery. An important issue was the Company's draft ordinances relating to the composition of the Company. Ordinance 6 in particular did not restrict membership to persons engaged in farming and ancillary trades, but was open to anyone whom the Court of Assistants saw fit to elect. Similarly membership of the Court was open to any member of the Company. The civic officials noted that there was 'nothing in the ordinances to preserve the existing craft character of the Company or to prevent control of the Company from passing into the hands of persons not engaged in farming and ancillary trades'. Ominously the civic officials' report noted 'as a general principle we would deprecate the granting of a livery to a transitory group of individuals, somewhat in the nature of a club, without an assured trade connection'.

Having received these inauspicious comments the General Purposes Committee voted in May 1951 not to proceed further with consideration of the Company's petition. Consultations took place behind the scenes regarding the draft ordinances and the Company made it known that it would be willing to redraft the ordinances to maintain a two-thirds majority of agricultural and allied trade membership of the Livery and the Court of Assistants. This suggestion was then passed back to the civic officials advising the General Purposes Committee who pointed out that an ordinance which restricted membership in this way would be unworkable in that it would not allow for the inevitable evolution of the membership caused by admissions to the Livery by patrimony and by the tendency of liverymen to change professions. The result would be to create two classes of members, which went against all custom and precedent of the established livery companies. In the end, after much cogitation on the problem of membership, a compromise was suggested which provided that the majority of the Court of Assistants should be persons engaged in farming. What type of majority was left un-stated and in the words of one of the City's officials 'if it leads to any ambiguities in the future, it can't be helped'. The larger issues behind the reluctance of the City Corporation are somewhat unclear but it appears as though there was some scepticism as to whether farmers were entitled to join the liveried traditions of the Square Mile. The net result of this opposition was months, and then the prospect of years, of delay.

The procrastination must have caused some disillusionment among the membership as several men wrote to the Clerk expressing their desire to resign from the Company. In some desperation the Clerk telephoned Sir Percy Greenaway prior to a meeting of the Company in mid-June 1951 asking for information as to the progress of the Company's petition. Sir Percy was unable to divulge any information due to the confidentiality of the proceedings, but the Clerk noted ominously 'reading between the lines it appeared that the petition was meeting with opposition'. Pending a result from the City Corporation, and no doubt hoping to demonstrate that they were actively pursuing their stated objectives, the Company decided to form an ad hoc committee to push forward its intention to set up a bursary for overseas visits by agricultural students.

At this stage the Company turned to King George VI for a helping hand. It was suggested by Lord Swaythling, that, in the light of the King's earlier letter of encouragement, enquiries should be made whether it might be possible 'to obtain further backing from the Palace'. The Master wrote to the King's Private Secretary, Sir Alan Lascelles, in neutral tones, explaining the Company's current position. In September 1951 the Company heard through Sir Ulick Alexander that the King was 'much interested to hear of the progress which has been made since the Company of Farmers was formed in 1947, and that a Petition for the Grant of a Livery is now under consideration by the General Purposes Committee of the City Corporation'. The King 'noted with interest' that should the Petition be acceded to, the Company of Farmers would be in a position to grant travelling scholarships. The Company put the communication from the Palace to immediate use, sending a copy to the Lord Mayor who had read it, reportedly 'with interest', before returning it to the Master.

A story told later suggests that the King's personal intervention proved crucial in influencing the City's response. George VI had learned of the slow progress through the Senior Warden Sir Richard Haddon who lived on a farm next to the Royal Farms at Windsor. After a chance meeting in Windsor Great Park Sir Richard told the King of the Company's difficulties. According to the manuscript history of the Company compiled by a long-standing member of the Company, Lt. Col. C. Attfield Brooks, 'The King thought for a moment and then said, "Leave it to me. I am dining with the Lord Mayor next week and will mention it to him casually." At the appropriate moment the next week the King turned to the Lord Mayor at the Guildhall Banquet saying, "By the way Lord Mayor, as a farmer myself I was delighted to learn that you are in the process of giving formal consideration to a request for a Grant of Livery to the Farmers Company. It will be a great pleasure to remember that it came about in your year of office.'"

The story is impossible to verify at this distance in time but no doubt the Farmers' Company had reasons to be grateful to the by then ailing monarch. The King's letter of support was rapidly followed by a positive response from the Court of Aldermen. On 22 January 1952 the General Purposes Committee delivered its report to the Court of Aldermen recommending that the Company's Petition be acceded to, subject to four conditions:

1. That the majority of the Court of Assistants shall be persons engaged in the farming industry.

2. That the Company shall take the necessary steps to constitute itself one in conformity with the Law and Custom of the City of London, and that its ordinances shall be approved by the Court of Aldermen.

3. That the number of the Livery shall not at any time exceed 250.

4. That the fee for Admission to the Livery shall be not less than 40 Guineas.

These changes to the Company's ordinances having been agreed to, the Court of Aldermen formally approved the Company's Grant of Livery on 10 June 1952. At a ceremony held at the Mansion House on 31 October 1952, the Lord Mayor, Sir Leslie Boyce, presented the formal Grant of Livery embodied in letters patent under the seal of the mayoralty and the Master accepted the illuminated vellum scroll. The event was filmed by British Gaumont News and three copies of the film given to the Company by its owner, Mr. J. Arthur Rank.* Through the kindness of the Lord Mayor it was arranged that the Company's fifth annual dinner—its first livery dinner— should be held at Mansion House in December 1952. A reception for the Commonwealth Prime Ministers visiting London for the Commonwealth Economic Conference was subsequently arranged to take place in the Guildhall on the same evening, and, of course, it was essential that the Lord Mayor and Sheriffs should be present at this function. Accordingly, the Company's first livery dinner was postponed to 7 January 1953.

Having crossed this crucial hurdle of obtaining formal recognition by the City Corporation, the Company set out to achieve its next important goal. A royal grant of a charter of incorporation was a necessary step to full corporate status and to give the Company the ability to hold investments and property in its own name. In

* A copy of the short film was deposited in the archives of the Corporation of London.

3   Presentation of the Grant of Livery to the Master, Lord Courthope, by the Lord Mayor, Sir Leslie Boyce, KBE, MA, on 31 October 1952. Also in the picture, from left, are: Alderman Sir Frank Newson-Smith (Lord Mayor 1943-44), Alderman Sir George Wilkinson Bt (Lord Mayor 1940-41) and Alderman Sir Percy Greenaway Bt (Lord Mayor 1932-33). (See p.89, illustration 50.)

contrast to its attempts to get a Grant of Livery, the Company's application for a Royal Charter went smoothly. After some alterations to the Company's ordinances, to gain the approval of the Privy Council, a Grant of Charter of Incorporation was formally made at Goodwood by Queen Elizabeth II on 29 July 1955. During the intervening period the Company began to take part in the round of ceremonial events which punctuate the official year in the City. In July 1953 it took its rightful place among the other livery companies at a river pageant on the Thames to mark the beginning of the new reign. That month the Court of the Company decided to hold a regular annual church service. Plans were also set in motion to implement further the Company's aims and objects through the sponsoring of agricultural education. By this time the Company could rightfully claim its place among the older established livery companies; if the preceding years were not without struggle it could face the future with some optimism.

Chapter Three

EDUCATION AND TRAINING

'The Advancement of Agricultural Education'

During the period that the Farmers were attempting to establish themselves as a *bona fide* Livery Company the founding members sought to define and implement its core activities. For centuries the London Livery Companies had acted as patrons and administrators of a wide array of educational institutions: grammar schools, university scholarships and lectureships. In addition to this the members of the Livery Companies were directly involved in the training and supervision of apprentices. The Courts of Assistants of the Companies examined apprentices in the secrets of their respective crafts, often requiring the production of a piece of work as evidence of their skill. Though this aspect of many of the Livery Companies' activities declined in the 19th century with the loss of their traditional responsibilities for the supervision of industry and trade, they became involved in technical training through the City and Guilds Institute, founded in 1873, which taught accredited courses in various trades.

The myriad of skills involved in farming the land was for centuries never part of any formal education or training. Farming and the rural crafts which went with it were 'bred' into the farmer and rural worker without recourse to examinations and paper qualifications. All this began to change towards the end of the 19th century. With the beginnings of the mechanisation of agriculture, and a greater degree of state involvement in the realms of training and education, the idea of formal training for farming began to take hold. From 1889 the Board of Agriculture began to provide limited assistance to agricultural education at existing schools and places of higher education. By the end of the century the Board of Agriculture encouraged the establishment of a network of agricultural colleges attached to established universities, including Wye College, which had been a medieval grammar school but became the South East College of Agriculture and was established in 1894 as the School of Agriculture of the University of London. Over the course of the first half of the 20th century this network gradually expanded with the setting up of farm institutes, grant aided agricultural colleges, county council agricultural advisory services and the expansion of agricultural teaching at the universities. Before, during and after the Second World War scientific research into agriculture became a matter of national importance, the expansion of production and increases in productivity being the main aims. Organisations such as the Nuffield Foundation, founded by the industrialist Lord Nuffield in 1943, sought to stimulate scientific research by means of cross-cultural exchanges. It was against this background that the nascent Farmers' Company became involved in agricultural education.

In November 1947 the Court of Assistants heard a number of proposals for expanding the Company's role in the area of training and education. The Master, Lord Courthope, recommended that the Company should consider the possibility of granting travelling bursaries 'on post graduate lines' for young people who had passed agricultural examinations. He suggested that, if the idea were to be taken up, then the British Dominions and United States might be included. Victor Parker further suggested that the Company become directly involved in providing scholarships to undergraduates studying for a degree in agriculture. Sir Cleveland Fyfe further proposed that the Company provide funds for post-graduate research. The Company heard from Sir Donald Vandepeer, Permanent Secretary at the Ministry of Agriculture, through a letter to Sir Richard Haddon, of the great benefits which had flowed from agricultural exchange programmes between Britain and the United States and Canada sponsored by the Nuffield Foundation since 1946 and suggesting that the Company sponsor a similar scheme for bringing young farmers from North America and sending young British farmers abroad. The positive publicity provided by the visit of six young British farmers to Ohio and of 22 Iowan farmers to Britain had helped to publicise the difficulties of post-war British agriculture. Such visits were expensive and difficult to mount, due to dollar shortages and the cost of transatlantic fares. Sir Donald suggested that the Company might provide assistance: 'there is a field of activity here which could be cultivated by the Company with great national advantage'. He also recommended that the Company sponsor apprenticeships for shepherds and grants for training thatchers. Education was emerging as a key area of the Company's future activities. In September 1949 the Company, in framing its petition to the City for official recognition as a livery company, formally committed itself to the principal aim of 'the advancement of education'.

Initially these plans did not get very far. The difficulties involved in obtaining the Grant of Livery and the Company's precarious finances precluded further progress. Though several meetings were held between 1947 and 1949 it was decided in March 1950 that further consideration should be deferred until the Grant of Livery had been obtained. By the end of 1950 it was reported that 'no tangible progress' could be made until the Company's financial position had improved. But Sir Richard Haddon, seeing that the City's attitude towards the Farmers would improve with some material commitment to achieving its formal aims, suggested that the Company should press ahead with plans for funding overseas exchanges. An *ad hoc* committee was set up to implement the Company's plans. Negotiations and consultations took place between the Company, the Ministry of Agriculture and the American Embassy. The scheme was mentioned in the Company's appeal to George VI for support in obtaining a Grant from the City. Two travelling bursaries, worth £1,800, were created in the later months of 1951. Two young farmers, R.D. Burdge and E.C.H. Chase, were selected and left home for a three-month tour of American farms in September 1952. But the scheme was relatively short-lived. Though the two young men submitted a report to the Company on their impressions of American agriculture which was circulated among the agricultural press, it was decided to suspend the bursaries in March 1953. This decision was made to enable the Company to consolidate its financial position. The Nuffield Foundation, which had started a similar scheme in 1946, was in the process of relinquishing the direct funding of its travelling bursaries for farmers and asking agricultural organisations to take on the responsibility for providing financial backing. So it was that in early 1955 the Company sat down with representatives of the Foundation along with delegates from the National Farmers' Union, the Milk Marketing Board, the Hops Marketing Board, the British Dairy Farmers' Association, the Bath and West Show, the Smithfield Club, the Royal Agricultural Society of England Show and Royal Counties Show and hammered out an agreement; each organisation agreed to undertake to sign a seven-year deed of covenant promising to pay £3,000 per annum in total to a fund to provide for overseas visits by young farmers to the U.S.A., Canada, Australia and New Zealand. The Company undertook a deed of covenant in March 1956 committing it to paying some £200 to the scheme. At the same time the Company also became involved in the nomination of candidates for the award of a travelling grant under the auspices of the English Speaking Union and the Ford Foundation. Thus by the mid-1950s the Company had, albeit modestly, striven to achieve its aims and to help in a small way to foster transatlantic and commonwealth cultural co-operation.

Apprenticeship: 'To learn the art of farming'

From the first years of its inception the Farmers' Company adopted the ancient method by which young people have been trained and admitted to the freedom of the Company and the City by means of a period of training. The seven-year apprenticeship or 'freedom by servitude' was for centuries one of the chief means of entry into the Livery Companies and freedom of the City, as well as the way in which trades and crafts were taught.

The revival of apprenticeship by the Farmers' Company was suggested in April

1947 by Sir Cleveland Fyfe. He proposed that the Company should compile a register of farmers willing to take on apprentices 'for the information of parents willing to apprentice their sons and/or daughters'. The Court of Assistants took up the idea and delegated Sir Richard Haddon to investigate. Because of the Company's difficulties in obtaining a Grant of Livery from the City Corporation the matter rested until April 1952 when the Clerk informed the Court of Assistants that 'one or two members had made enquiries about the possibility of apprenticing their sons to members of the Company'. In response to these enquiries the Clerk said that, when the Grant of Livery was formally handed over, apprentices could be taken by any member for a period of not less than four years and not more than eight years and that, on completion of the period of apprenticeship, the apprentice could be admitted to the Company. The Clerk was asked to draw attention to this procedure when circulating this information to the members of the Livery and by November 1952 several members had asked for the particulars of binding apprentices. At the time it was decided to fix the fines payable at the start and completion of the apprenticeship at two guineas and four guineas. During discussions a number of the Court expressed the view that apprentices admitted to the Company should be 'working apprentices'. This opinion found its way into the series of recommendations and a draft form of indenture for apprenticeships was drawn up by Nevill Matthews with the assistance of the Chamberlain of the City in September 1953. Among other suggestions Nevill Matthews recommended that, subject to the discretion of the Court of Assistants, apprentices were to be restricted to those who intended to 'learn the art of farming or one of the ancillary interests of agriculture'. A form of a ceremony for binding the apprentice, which involved the presentation of a bible embossed with the Company's arms and the delivery of a few appropriate words by the master, was drawn up in consultation with the Clerk of the Worshipful Company of Goldsmiths.

By the end of 1953 a list of some six members of the Company desiring to apprentice their sons, including Nevill Matthews himself, was put forward. The Court thought the list 'a most encouraging one'. On the morning of 8 June 1954 Guy Matthews, son of Nevill Matthews, was duly brought before the Senior Warden, Victor Parker (deputising in the absence of the Master Sir Richard Haddon), along with William Cumber, the Junior Warden, at Innholders' Hall and duly bound as apprentice to his father. After signing the necessary documentation the new apprentice was welcomed by the Senior Warden and presented with a copy of the bible. The Company's Chaplain, the Reverend Cyril Cresswell, had composed a few words which, in eloquent tones, underscored the spiritual basis which gave meaning to guild life: '… to keep you ever mindful of the Law and the Gospel of God as the rule for your whole life and calling I present you with this Book, the most valuable thing that this world affords … Here is Wisdom; This is the Royal Law. These are the lively oracles of God.'

Thus was a pattern set by which young men (and more recently women) committed themselves to the service of their masters along lines established in the earliest history of the Livery Companies. Over the next ten years some 20 young men stepped forward to become apprentices to the Company. In each instance the Court took great care to ascertain that the prospective apprentice actually intended to go into farming, in one case holding up an application when it was found that the young man's father was both a farmer and a solicitor. In the large majority of cases apprentices have been bound to their fathers. In December 1959 one such young man, Arnold Quinney Hitchcock, became the first apprentice to have completed his indentures and be admitted to the Livery. He became Master of the Company in 1978. Since these early days 'freedom by servitude' has been an important means by which the bonds between parents and children have been strengthened, and by which new members of the Company have come forward.

Wye College and the Folkestone Experiment

What was to become a long-standing and fruitful association with Wye College, University of London, began very modestly in the mid-1950s. In September 1956 an enthusiastic new member of the Court of Assistants, Ernest Geoffrey Parsons, a Wiltshire farmer, Crown Estate Commissioner and one-time Chairman of that county's Agricultural Executive Committee, wrote to the Master and Wardens with the proposal that the Company establish a lecture, to be named in honour of Lord Courthope, to be held in London and which would be for the benefit of both the members of the Company and the wider agricultural community. This proposal contained in embryo the ideas that would form the Company's involvement with Wye College:

> I would respectfully suggest that a Livery Company so closely connected with the great business centre of the City of London could do no better than undertake the study and discussion of business management as it applies to agriculture in its widest sense, embracing farm management, time and motion study, buildings, forestry, aspects of capital and tax, and so on.

The Company took up Geoffrey Parsons' idea of an annual lecture, though not initially along the lines which he had envisaged. An *ad hoc* committee consisting of Geoffrey Parsons, Nevill Matthews, and Past Master Victor Parker met and recommended that a trial lecture be held following one of the Company's annual Court Luncheons. The Chamberlain of London was invited to deliver a lecture on the Livery Companies after which the audience of liverymen would be consulted to see whether the idea of an annual lecture should be continued and expanded.

The lecture by the Chamberlain of London went ahead in 1957 and a lecture was presented the next year by one of the Brethren of Trinity House but the idea of a lecture on farm business management remained on the table. The Company's involvement with Wye College came several years later during the year of Mastership of Thomas Neame, who was a member of the governing body of the College. In June 1959 Liveryman Edward Partridge relayed to the Master a communication he had received from B. J. Furneaux, a governor of the college, about the possibility of the Company sponsoring an award to be given to outstanding graduates. The Worshipful Company of Fruiterers, a Company founded in 1625, already presented an annual medal and a £5 prize and the College was apparently eager to involve the Company in a similar scheme. The Governors of the College expressed the view that 'it would be a most graceful gesture if the Court were to see fit to make some award to the College at the conclusion of Thomas Neame's Mastership, seeing that he is a most valued member of the Governing Body of the College, being appointed to it by the Royal Agricultural Society'. The Company took up the invitation to sponsor an award of a silver gilt medal to be given to a student completing a General or Honours B.Sc. degree in Agriculture* who was adjudged by the College on general performance throughout the course 'to show the greatest aptitude for work in farm management combined with a good general level of attainment in both academic and practical work'. The first medal was awarded in December 1960 to John McInerney (later to become Professor of Agricultural Economics at Exeter University) who thanked the Company with the wish that '… May your Company continue to grow and thrive in the common interest of agriculture'. The young student's fulsome sentiments, recorded in the Company's Court Minutes, must have provided a powerful boost to the Company's ambitions to extend its activities in the educational sphere.

The decision to expand the range of the Company's direct involvement with Wye College came through the intervention of Geoffrey Parsons, who showed the same enthusiasm with which he had previously advocated the idea of the annual 'Courthope Lecture'. Derek Pearce, a young farm manager at the 8,000-acre Frederick Hiam farm near Cambridge who had been sponsored by Geoffrey Parsons to attend the prestigious Harvard Business School, relates how discussions with his sponsor, who was non-executive director of Frederick Hiam, led to the idea of a form of business training in farm management. At a meeting of the Court of Assistants in June 1961 just after his election as Junior Warden, Parsons made it known that 'he wished to propose that this Court gives further consideration to the Aims & Objects of our Company' particularly the commitment to training young farmers at home and overseas'. He told

---

* This medal is now awarded for excellence in Agricultural Business Management as well.

the Court meeting that he appreciated 'our limited resources but our Company was made up of men of vast knowledge with international interests' and he felt confident that 'we should all be willing to use our experience and resources to further the training of the limited number of the most able young men wishing to enter the Industry and who will eventually contribute to a vast business expansion inevitable in the future'. The response of members of the Court to this intervention was not immediately enthusiastic. Past Master Victor Parker cautioned against any expansion in the Company's involvement, reminding the Court that it had abandoned the direct financing of overseas exchanges in favour of a Deed of Covenant which channelled funds into the scheme run by the Nuffield Foundation. This contribution, Victor Parker felt, meant that the 'Company was getting the best results at the cheapest costs'.

Despite these sentiments, the Senior Warden, Stephen Cheveley, suggested that Geoffrey Parsons prepare a memorandum on the subject for further consideration. By December he had produced a short memorandum to the Court outlining proposals for a scheme of postgraduate training in farm management. A more elaborate plan of action, based on Geoffrey Parsons' original proposals, was produced by Stephen Cheveley, by then elected Master, after discussions with Dr. Harold Saunders, Chief Scientist, Ministry of Agriculture Fisheries and Food and latterly Professor of Agriculture, Reading University, who had pronounced that such a scheme would, in his words, 'break new ground'. The Master, Stephen Cheveley, described the need for a scheme specifically focusing on the application of modern business principles to farm management, something which the existing University undergraduate curriculum could cover only superficially. A 14-week course for six students including residential study at different agricultural research centres as well as group visits to farms was proposed. At this stage it was envisaged that students would move from one centre to another over the course with the established centres at Reading, Cambridge, Wye, Seale Hayne, Leeds and Aberdeen being mentioned. Candidates were to be rigorously selected from amongst those who already had practical experience of farming but who were destined for jobs in farm management. The cost was estimated to be some £2,100 which might be partially borne by the Farmers' Company and perhaps commercial firms. After discussion, during which the suggestion of commercial involvement was objected to, it was decided that an *ad hoc* committee on the scheme be formed under the leadership of Geoffrey Parsons in consultation with the Master to give consideration to the practical means by which it could be implemented.

The scheme thereafter rapidly began to take shape with the Master, Stephen Cheveley, who had himself been in receipt of a Ministry of Agriculture scholarship at Leeds University after the Great War, taking a decisive role. Special meetings of the Court of Assistants were held in May and July 1962 to discuss the proposal.

Objections were voiced both to the cost involved and the supposedly narrow focus on postgraduate farm management but it was then agreed that the Company should devote its attention to what came to be called the 'Advanced Course in Farm Business Management'. It was decided to approach the Nuffield Foundation Trust for its views on the scheme as well as possible financial assistance. The promise of some financial assistance depended on the contribution of members of the Company both to the financial backing and the planning of the scheme. Representatives of the Nuffield Foundation expressed the view that the scheme was 'highly promising … it seemed to provide an excellent example of an industry and its members contributing both individually and collectively to the well being of that industry'. Eventually some £1,500 was pledged by the Nuffield Foundation to make up the estimated £2,100 cost of operating the courses, the remainder being made up by voluntary contributions from members of the Livery.

It was from this point that the Company began to focus on Wye College as the appropriate institutional base for its courses. In Spring 1962 members of the Court—including Past Masters Stephen Cheveley and Sir Thomas Neame, with Junior Warden Geoffrey Parsons and Assistants Peter Taylor and Edward Hitchcock—visited Wye College and engaged in discussion with the Principal, Dunstan Skilbeck and Ian Reid about the running of the course. The latter, as a Senior Lecturer at the College, was currently responsible for the development of a course leading to the Academic Postgraduate Diploma in Farm Business Administration. Wye College, as part of the University of London, was felt to be highly appropriate for a City of London Livery Company to cultivate as an ally in the promotion of agricultural education. Because of shortages in accommodation it was decided that the courses should be held under the aegis of Wye College but at the *Clifton Hotel*, Folkestone. The proposed course was scaled down to three weeks. A syllabus consisting of lectures and practical farm visits covering planning, management accounting, finance, taxation, labour management, work-study and animal and crop husbandry was laid down. The first course was held at Folkestone at the end of January 1963. An important element of the course was the active participation of Company members and lectures were provided by, amongst others, Past Master Stephen Cheveley and Sir Thomas Neame. The course was modelled on 'Dipl. FBA' and subsequently incorporated ideas and teaching methods learnt by Derek Pearce and Ian Reid from their participation in short courses run by the prestigious Harvard Business School. The Folkestone Experiment was a forerunner of the Continuing Professional Development Programme which now forms a major activity in the work of Wye College.

The course, attended by some eight students, was judged an immediate success, though no plans had been made for the future. It was soon realised that the courses should be put on a more secure financial footing. It was decided that the Company's deed of covenant of 1956, which committed it to paying out funds to the Nuffield travelling bursaries, should be altered to allow the Company to devote part of its income from sources such as quarterage fees, collections at Company meetings and other sources towards the Wye course. At the same time it was decided to raise the quarterage fees by two guineas in order to garner further income and to require that students attending the course make a nominal contribution to its running costs. Other possible sources of income were also contemplated. Importantly for the future development of the Company, it was in this context that Walter Cardy, a member of the Court, suggested in December 1963 that the Company provide itself with a capital structure which would enable it to 'broaden its activities' by means of constructing a livery hall, as part of a commercial development, which would yield revenue for the future. Though it was to be many years before this suggestion was realised, a committee was set up to consider the matter. In the meantime an educational trust fund was set up to channel funds to the course and via appeals to the Livery the Company's share of the running costs was made up.

Among the individual acts of generosity by members of the Company during the early running of the Folkestone experiment was a gift of £500 by Philip Henman, founder of the Transport Development Group, who farmed in Surrey and Scotland and who had joined the Company in 1958. Mr. Henman was to be a munificent supporter of the Company during these years and the source of much useful financial advice. For his great generosity Henman was later elected as honorary member of the Court of Assistants and served as Chairman of the Company's Finance Committee for several years. By its third year the Folkestone Experiment was well established, with Ian Reid taking a leading role in the academic running of the course, ably assisted as Senior Tutor by Edgar Thomas, recently retired from the Chair of Agricultural Economics, Reading University, and under whom Ian Reid had worked before going to Wye. Michael Cheveley, the son of Past Master Stephen Cheveley and a member of the first course in 1963, took charge of the general administration of the course. Numbers attending the course expanded to 18 and over the next ten years more than three hundred men attended. In addition to farmers, land agents, bankers and men from ancillary businesses were brought in to the course. In order to broaden the geographical coverage of the courses the Company decided in 1968 to run a concentrated course at Hexham, to begin just after Christmas 1969 under the auspices of the University of Newcastle's School of Agriculture. After difficulties were experienced with the timing, costs and control of the course, the scheme was dropped and the money thus saved was redirected to running two courses per year at Folkestone, one beginning in November and the other beginning in January. In this context it should be recorded that in 1974 the then immediate Past Master Leslie Barker was tragically killed in a car accident returning from addressing a re-union of members of the Hexham course. The two courses ran at Folkestone until March 1975 when it was decided, because of difficulties in obtaining suitable facilities, to move the courses to Wye College. Due to problems experienced with running a course so close to Christmas, it was decided in June 1979 to hold one course only in January. By the early 1970s some 36 places were available. In 1973 as a result of informal discussions between the then Master, Ronald Borner, and the Administrator of the Trustees of the MacRobert Trusts, the trustees donated some £800 per annum to provide four places on the Wye course to Scottish farmers. Since that time the courses have been a great success. After some 37 years down the line they are continually oversubscribed. In addition former members of the courses have been an important source of new recruits and a means by which the farming community has gained new lifeblood. The course is on a sound financial footing thanks to contributions from candidates and grants with support of the Lord Lonsdale Trust, the Geoffrey and Ilsa Parsons Trust and other supporters.

A 'Community of Minds': The Centre for European Agricultural Studies

By the time the Folkestone initiative had been in operation for almost a decade British agriculture was on the verge of undergoing the most radical transformation since the end of the Second World War. The resignation of General de Gaulle in 1969 and the election of the government of Edward Heath in June 1970 opened the door to Britain's entry into the European Economic Community, long delayed due to French opposition. As negotiations were underway members of the Company began to see the need to involve the Farmers' Company in some, albeit small, way. At the end of 1970 Students from EEC countries, one from the Netherlands and one from Germany, were invited to take part in the Folkestone course, with funding from the Ernest Cook Trust. In March 1971 Past Master Stephen Cheveley made a short statement to the Court of Assistants regarding discussions he had had with Dunstan Skilbeck and Ian Reid about the implications of entry into the Common Market. Together they had formed the view, in Stephen Cheveley's words, 'that the government was concerned only with the political aspects. It was appreciated that British farmers had to safeguard their own interests but, at the same time, British farmers could contribute a great deal of knowledge to the European Community, and, in addition, there was a great deal which we could learn from farmers in the E.E.C. countries'. He considered that there was a need to create, as he put it, a 'Community of Minds' to exchange information on matters such as the use of land, the social aspects of agriculture, and technology and finance in farming. To this end, Stephen Cheveley and Dunstan Skilbeck proposed that the Company should help to arrange a meeting of interested parties, perhaps with the assistance of the Ernest

Cook Trust. The Court reacted cautiously to the suggestion, authorising him to go ahead with the proposed meeting, favouring, as it was put, 'exploration without commitment'. Later that year it was decided that no more could be done until it was certain that Britain would enter the EEC. The Treaty of Accession—committing Britain along with the Irish Republic and Denmark to joining the Common Market—was signed in January 1972.

Stephen Cheveley's intervention provided the germ of an idea which was to be realised in permanent form at Wye College over the following few years. By spring 1972 the idea of establishing a Centre for European Agricultural Studies (CEAS) at Wye College had been mooted at a Court of Assistants meeting and by July that year the governing body of Wye College had given its formal backing for the proposed Centre. The primary aim of the Centre was to give a permanent forum for Stephen Cheveley's 'Community of Minds': a residential centre which would provide a venue for the exchange of ideas and the development of information among European agriculturists, farmers, government officials, businessmen and academics in an atmosphere, as Stephen Cheveley put it, 'free from political and nationalistic pressures'.

Given the ambitious scope of the centre it was realised early on that the resources of the Company could not possibly meet the entire cost. An elaborate appeal scheme was mobilised under the leadership of Stephen Cheveley, now the senior Past Master. A target figure of £500,000 was set and approaches were made to the Ministry of Agriculture and the Department of Education, the University of London and the University Grants Committee. These bodies gave a warm welcome to the idea of establishing the Centre. The Appeal Committee, set up by the Company in August 1972, sounded out the possibility of state financial assistance and when this proved not to be forthcoming the Committee was compelled to seek a wide range of outside support. The personal connections of many of the Company were used to garner aid. Stephen Cheveley's previous incarnation as head of ICI's agricultural division proved particularly useful as a source of contacts. His mixture of Irish charm and Yorkshire grit could, it was said, 'get money out of stones'. The Appeal Committee was widened to include members of the Governing Body of Wye College plus several distinguished figures from both the worlds of business and agriculture. Among the individuals and organisations represented on the Appeals Committee were the Duke of Northumberland, Chairman of the Council of the Royal Agricultural Society and a Liveryman since 1948, Professor C.H. Phillips, Vice Chancellor of the University of London, John D. Sainsbury, Chairman of Sainsbury Ltd., Sir Henry Plumb, President of the National Farmers Union, Dr. S. Mansholt, formerly Agricultural Commissioner of the European Economic Commission, Dr. S. Koechlin, Managing Director of Ciba-Giegy, of Switzerland, and Lord Melchett, Chairman of British Steel Corporation who was also a farmer and landowner. The Company was

4   Launch of the appeal for the Centre for European Agricultural Studies at the Farmers' Club on 21 June 1973. *From left to right*: Immediate Past Master, Frank Garner; Chairman of the Governors of Wye College, Sir Richard Boughey; President of the National Farmers' Union, Sir Henry Plumb; Governor of Wye College, Sir Nigel Strutt; Principal of Wye College, Dr. Harry Darling; The Master, Ronald Borner; Past Master and Governor of Wye College, Stephen Cheveley; President of the Country Landowners' Association, Sir Charles Graham; Professor Denis Britton.

represented by the then Master, Ronald Borner, Past Master Frank Garner, latterly Principal of the Royal Agricultural College, Cirencester, and Past Masters Herbert Graves, J.K. Knowles and Arnold Hitchcock, with Stephen Cheveley acting as Chairman of the Committee in his capacity as a Governor of Wye College. A fund-raising and publicity firm was appointed and a campaign secretary installed at Wye College. Ian Reid, who had been so crucial to the running of the Advanced Farm Business Management Course, was appointed as the Director of the Centre. Up to this point the Committee made only informal enquiries about contributions to the Appeal. These proved promising with some £89,000 being promised from, amongst others, Wye College itself, which offered £50,000 by May 1973. The Appeal 'went public' at a press conference held on 21 June that year at the Farmers' Club, hosted by the Master, Ronald Borner. The launch of the appeal was supported by the Presidents of the National Farmers Union, the Country Landowners' Association and the Chairman of Governors of Wye College. By the end of that year some £100,000 had been raised, 48 members of the Company contributing £32,000 and

5   At Mansion House on
6 March 1974. The Lord
Mayor, Sir Hugh Wontner,
with Her Majesty Queen
Elizabeth, the Queen
Mother and the Master, the
Earl of Lonsdale, on the
occasion of the Appeal for
the Centre for European
Agricultural Studies at Wye
College.

a separate appeal launched among members of the Farmers' Club raising over
£3,500. These sums, it was reported in the Appeals Committee's first progress
report, 'effectively answer the critics who said that the farmers would not support
the centre'. The Appeals Committee's efforts culminated in a public reception held
at Mansion House on 6 March 1974 which was attended by Her Majesty Queen
Elizabeth the Queen Mother, the Lord Mayor and Sheriffs, several Ambassadors
from E.E.C. countries and a number of eminent guests from industry and the
agricultural world. The Master, the Earl of Lonsdale, welcomed Her Majesty the
Queen Mother. The reception both formally announced the establishment of the
Centre as well as acting as a springboard for raising further donations to the Appeal.
The event, held by courtesy of the then Lord Mayor, Sir Hugh Wontner, was a great
success. By the time of the reception some £380,000 had been raised of which
approximately £100,000 had come through members of the Company.

Despite this generosity problems arose. The rate of inflation increased rapidly
through 1974 to an annual rate of 9.26 per cent, exacerbated by the worldwide oil
crisis and the parlous state of the British economy. By June of that year it was

realised that the original projected sum of £500,000 would have to be revised to £600,000. In November a further £50,000 was added to the projected cost. Amidst this the re-election in February 1974 of the government of Harold Wilson, who had campaigned on the promise of a referendum on Britain's membership of the E.E.C., ushered in a period of uncertainty over the Centre's future. Despite this plans for the Centre went ahead. An interim Council of Management (which included Past Masters Stephen Cheveley, Herbert Graves and Frank Garner as well as the then Master, the Earl of Lonsdale) was set up in early 1974. The Appeals Committee continued its efforts, with some £430,000 being raised by November 1974. Ian Reid and a small staff meanwhile began to undertake research work into the various aspects of British and European agriculture, including the development of agricultural co-operatives undertaken for the European Commission and a joint study with the University of Padua of family farms. Initially housed in temporary accommodation in a converted garage, work began in July 1974 on the first phase of the building of the Centre. On 30 September 1974 the foundation stone of the Centre was laid by the Duke of Northumberland. Despite roaring inflation and the cloud of uncertainty posed by the referendum campaign the Centre was fast nearing completion. A well-appointed lecture theatre, with facilities for simultaneous translation, seminar rooms and a library were constructed. These were named after the major donors, the Frank Parkinson Trust, Sir John Sainsbury and Lord Rank respectively. An intriguing mural representing the produce of the various E.E.C. member states was commissioned from the artist Gordon Davies and funded by the Abbey Trust. Within a year of the foundation stone laying ceremony the Centre was officially opened on 20 September 1975 by Sir Henry Plumb, President of the National Farmers' Union (Lord Plumb, 1987) and President of the Comité des Organisations Professionelles Agricoles (COPA) and by Cornelis Knotterus, past President of COPA and an important figure in European agriculture. As a mark of the truly European nature of the enterprise the opening ceremony was attended by a full Praesidium of COPA. This sense of international collaboration was commemorated in the planting of nine young saplings each representing one of the E.E.C. member states and planted by its incumbent Agricultural Attaché. George Foster, the Irish Attaché, watered in his Killarney Strawberry tree with bottles of Guinness.

Since its opening the Centre has sought to play a full part in the development of co-operation in European agriculture. A European Documentation Centre, bringing together studies and publications on European agriculture, was established at the Centre's Lord Rank Library together with funding from the Worshipful Company of Fruiterers. CEAS has striven to act as an impartial forum for top-level discussions through seminars, conferences and courses. The academic staff of CEAS have produced a wealth of research reports, publications and studies on all aspects of the farming industry, and agricultural policy in Britain, Europe and the wider world. The Centre has had to fight and win a place in the sometimes harsh environment of higher education and research. Because of cutbacks in the early 1980s the Centre's outstation at Montpelier had to be scaled down. Amidst diminishing state aid for universities it was decided to split the academic research element from the Centre's consultancy work. In 1986 the College established a joint-venture with Produce Studies Ltd. as CEAS Consultants (Wye) Ltd. The rent it pays for the accommodation at the Centre is channelled into the funding of research fellowships and in part provides funds for the tuition fees of students on the Advanced Farm Business Management Course. The Advanced Farm Business Management Course was the forerunner and now is an integral part of the Continuing Professional Development (C. P. D.) Programme. This programme now embraces over 1,000 students from some 100 foreign countries and covers the whole panoply of agriculture, the food industry and the natural environment. It will continue as a major integrating activity with the merger of Wye College with Imperial College, University of London, which was agreed in 1999. In 1991, in order to honour the contribution of Stephen Cheveley to the establishment of CEAS, two rooms were designated as 'the Cheveley Rooms'. In the early 1980s the Common Agricultural Policy (CAP) came under increasing pressure from the farmers of North America and the Antipodes. It was therefore

6   The first course in Advanced Farm Business Management held at Folkestone in 1963. *Seated, from left to right*: Past Master, Sir Thomas Neame; Past Master, Stephen Cheveley; G.H. Pinney; The Master, Lord Swaythling; T. Woodhead; Senior Warden, Geoffrey Parsons; Assistant, Edward Hitchcock; Assistant, Walter Cardy. *Standing, from left to right*: Mr. Lindsay, Administrator; T.A. Woodhead; A.C. Cumming; M.C. Cheveley; G. Wilson; T.J. Calcutt; C.D. Neame; G.O. Hector; Ian Reid, Course Director, see also illustration 9.

decided in 1985 to offer a place on the Wye course to a Nuffield Scholar coming from the US, Canada, Australia or New Zealand. Such participation has been significant and enlivening. It has meant that the Company has been able to repay the support it received in its early days from the Nuffield Foundation.

It is worth considering the scope of the work of the CEAS Appeals Committee and the Company's contribution to it. In all some 134 different companies, organisations and trusts, including some of British industry's best known household names, had given funds for the Centre. Money came from organisations and bodies large and small including charitable trusts, private firms, agricultural co-operatives, agricultural trade associations, firms of land agents and valuers and the City Livery Companies. Food industry and agrichemical firms were particularly well

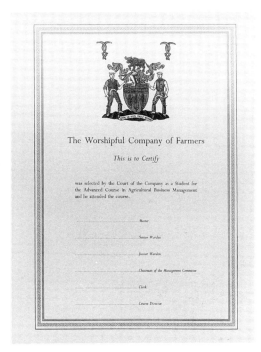

The Worshipful Company of Farmers

This is to Certify

was selected by the Court of the Company as a Student for the Advanced Course in Agricultural Business Management and he attended the course.

Master

Senior Warden

Junior Warden

Chairman of the Management Committee

Clerk

Course Director

7 The Agricultural Business Management Certificate awarded to all candidates successfully completing the Agricultural Business Management Course.

represented as donors to the Appeal. Amongst the Livery Companies forthcoming with support were the Goldsmiths, Butchers, Innholders, Fletchers, Fruiterers, Needlemakers, Wheelwrights, Glass-sellers and Launderers. In addition some 72 members of the Farmers' Company gave money directly to the appeal. Such a wide range of support, mobilised by what was then a relatively new livery company, recalled the original spirit that had animated the founders of the Farmers' Company in the mid-1940s. Then, at the end of a devastating European and worldwide conflict, the aim had been to perpetuate a spirit of war-time co-operation. By the mid-1970s, at a time of peaceful European integration, a similar sense of co-operation was being realised, albeit in very different circumstances.

The Company's support for education was not limited to its involvement with Wye. Building on its early support for cross-cultural educational exchanges the Company extended its support to various travelling scholarship schemes. In June 1965 Senior Warden Walter Cardy suggested that the Farmers' Company should form an association with the Australian Young Farmers Association who were sponsored by the P. & O. Line to send six of their members who travelled free on the SS. Canberra on scholarship visits to Britain every year. It was decided later that year to invite the six Australians as guests to the Company's Court Luncheon along with the Chairman of the P.& O. Line. This annual invitation was extended over the next three years until in mid-1968 Past Master Walter Cardy put forward the proposal to enrol the visiting farmers as yeomen of the Company with a view towards their eventual enrolment as Freemen. He generously offered £500 as recognition of his year of office, the interest on which and the capital if necessary to be used to foster this association. The Company accepted Past Master Cardy's proposal and the support for the 'Canberra Awards', as the scheme came to be known, continued for several years until 1973 when the P. & O. line discontinued the scholarships. In 1972 Philip Henman, who had already supported the Company's efforts at Wye, decided to mark

8   The first course in the Challenge of Rural Leadership at Seale Hayne, University of Plymouth, November 1996. *Seated left to right*: Stephen Fisher, Senior Lecturer; Richard Soffe, Course Tutor and Senior Lecturer; Philip Gibbons, Assistant Chairman of the Education Committee; Ewen Cameron, President, Country Landowners' Association; Marcus Cornish, Master; John Borner, Immediate Past Master; Michael Dart, Liveryman; John Cossins, Assistant; Martyn Warren, Head of Rural Land Use and Rural Management, University of Plymouth.

9   50th course in Agricultural Business Management, 21 January 2000. *Back row, from left to right*:
Prof. P. Webster; Hans Jorgensen; Jaco Burgers; George Jessel; James Griffiths; Dean Johns;
Duncan Blyth; Bruce Mackie; Iain Brown. *Middle row, from left to right*: Stephen Alderman; Simon
Madge; Ed Jones; Assistant Nick Fiske; Simon Meyrick; John Service; Andrew Wreathall; Ian
Reid. *Front row, from left to right*: Lorraine Pope; Martin Coward; Paul Broughton; The Master,
John Cossins; Catherine Suckley; Nicola Madeley; Stewart Watt. See also illustration 6.

his esteem for the Company by giving £15,000 to the Company's Charitable Fund to
assist young men and women to gain practical experience to assist them with their
agricultural or horticultural careers. A special emphasis was to be placed on funding
travelling scholarships to enable young people to gain practical experience overseas.
The Henman Award was intended, in Philip Henman's words, 'to help people who
were either involved or intending to be involved in farming and would help them to
prepare for such a calling' with the proviso that 'the fund was not to be used for the
purpose of general education'. This sum was generously supplemented by a further
£10,000 from Mr. Henman in 1982.

Another generous gift came in 1987 when Past Master Geoffrey Parsons, who had been a prime mover in the development of the Wye Courses, and his wife Ilsa, set up a trust worth some £30,000 to further the development of agricultural and farm business management through the courses at Wye College and for adult education.

Thus the Company's support for a variety of educational schemes has helped to advance its original goals. The Company's educational efforts have concentrated on providing innovative educational experiments in promoting the latest techniques and ideas in modern agriculture, while at the same time promoting a broader understanding and international co-operation in agriculture at a time when older associations such as the Commonwealth were being augmented by newer ties with Europe.[*]

---

[*] For the Company's most recent endeavours in education see below p.91.

Chapter Four

CHARITY, HOSPITALITY AND GOOD WORKS

Introduction

Charity, hospitality, collective acts of worship and participation in civic ceremonies have long played an important part of the life of the City Livery Companies. For centuries the Livery Companies have provided succour for the poor, administering charitable bequests, almshouses and schools. Individual members of the Livery Companies since their inception have been brought together at church services, banquets and public occasions, in which all the solemnity and regalia of guild membership have been displayed. In the early years, between the Grant of Livery and the establishment of the Folkestone Course, the Farmers' Company sought to take up these traditions of civic life; building a proud legacy of benevolence to good causes, attendance at church services at some of the most venerable parish churches of the City of London, welcoming visitors to the City and taking part in the yearly round of official ceremonies and celebrations which mark the civic year. Through these activities the Farmers' Company has promoted links between the country and town and between agriculture and the wider world.

'God Speed the Plough': Church Services

One of the oldest traditions of the City livery companies was the annual attendance of church services on saints' days and other points in the Christian calendar. This calendar, geared to the agricultural year for centuries, linked the worlds of the city and the country. The ancient tradition of celebrating the end of the harvest with singing, Corn Dollies and harvest 'Kerns' or suppers was a custom which was long marked on Britain's fields and farms in the days before mechanisation. In 1843 the Revd. R.S. Hawker, vicar of Morwenstow, in Cornwall, revived the ancient thanksgiving service of Lamas and this custom spread widely and became part of the established liturgy. Harvest festivals were particularly popular in the City in the post-war years when the parish churches were being reconstructed, and, once rationing had come to an end, the City's meat, fish and produce markets started to resume normal business.

As the Company struggled to establish its official status the spiritual side of the Company's affairs had to await material developments. But this did not prevent the Master, Lord Courthope, from accepting the invitation of the Friends of Canterbury Cathedral to attend a 'Harvest Festival of the World' to mark the opening of the Canterbury Festival. As the Company became more established it took tentative steps in participating in collective acts of worship. In March 1949 Richard Haddon suggested that the Company appoint an Honorary Chaplain to the Company. He recommended a young clergyman who farmed 300 acres near Guildford, the Revd. Cyril Cresswell, Chaplain of the King's Chapel of the Savoy. The Revd. Cresswell, who kept Guernsey and Shorthorn herds, was, according to Richard Haddon, 'terribly keen on farming' and would make 'an ideal Padre' for the Company. Lord Courthope thought the suggestion was 'excellent' and the Revd. Cresswell was appointed Chaplain in 1950. The new Chaplain approached the Court about the possibility of holding an annual service but the Court decided to postpone consideration until the Company had received a Grant of Livery. The weighty negotiations with the City Corporation diverted attention and inevitably caused delay.

Later that year, 1950, the Clerk represented the Company at a service of Thanksgiving for the Nation's Harvest held at St Paul's Cathedral. In June 1951 the Chaplain suggested to Sir Richard Haddon that a service of thanksgiving be sponsored by the Company just before the Smithfield Show when a large number of the Livery would be in London. The idea of service of thanksgiving was passed to the Committee appointed to deal with the aims and objects of the Company. By September 1951 the Master felt confident to suggest that the Revd. Cresswell should be elected as an honorary Liveryman, 'the Company now getting into a settled position'. Despite this the weighty negotiations with the City Corporation over the Grant of Livery and the attempt to set up the bursary scheme meant that the Company took no action for two years, until September 1953, when the Court instituted annual church services at St Stephen Walbrook prior to the Company's annual Livery Dinner. St Stephen Walbrook was one of Sir Christopher Wren's more famous churches, footsteps from the Mansion House, which had been badly damaged in the Blitz of 1940. After restoration, it became the Company's home church in its early years. Its minister during the early 1960s was the Revd. Chad Varah, charismatic founder of the Samaritans, who deputised for Cyril Cresswell on many occasions. A regular sight during the Company's association with St Stephen's was its annual procession in dinner dress to Mansion House. In 1973 it was decided to shift the venue of the annual church service to the church of St Mary at Hill, off Eastcheap, where the Company remained until the late 1980s.

In addition to the annual church service the Company also participated in the revival of the tradition of the harvest festival. The main charitable body associated

10   The Beadle, John South, leading the Master, Wardens and Court in procession to the Harvest Festival Service at St Bartholomew's Church on 4 October 1999. *From left to right*: Deputy Master, Past Master, Simon Taylor; Past Master, Andrew Streeter; HRH The Princess Royal; the Hon. Mrs. Louloudis, Lady in Waiting, behind; Senior Past Master, Ronald Borner; the Clerk, Margaret Winter; Junior Warden, Richard Brooks; Master Christopher Pertwee, wearing the brown quilted velvet cap made and presented by Miss Amy Streeter, Apprentice; Senior Warden, John Cossins; the Beadle is carrying the Mace.

with the Corn Exchange, the Corn Exchange Benevolent Society, set about reviving a service of thanksgiving at All Hallows-by-the-Tower and in summer 1954 the Company was invited to take part in a service in October, to be attended by the Lord Mayor and the Sheriffs. Later the Court heard that the service had been 'most impressive'. About this time the idea of holding a City Harvest Thanksgiving service was mooted by the Revd. Chad Varah. In a letter to the Company in March 1955 the Revd. Varah proposed a service to be held at St Stephen's, 'the right place for a City Harvest Thanksgiving, as it was the Church of the Farmers, Fruiterers and Carmen, all of whom are concerned with the production and distribution of our daily food'. In addition the Revd. Varah was acting as Chaplain to the Bakers' Company and was hoping that he would be able to get them to participate. The Revd. Cresswell investigated this possibility and produced an extensive report to the Company on the subject in March 1956. It stated that there was an increasing number of restored churches holding their own parish festivals. In addition several trade organisations as well as the City's main produce markets held their own unique harvest festivals. The Chaplain felt that a separate harvest festival organised by the Company might detract from the other festivals and that this might 'cause feeling'. In the end the Company decided to continue to celebrate the harvest in conjunction with the Corn Exchange Benevolent Fund and this tradition continued for many years. During this time the Company's Chaplain on occasion was called upon to give the address at the service. In 1963 Sir Thomas Neame, who was famed for his Kentish orchards, offered to donate a quantity of fruit to the service. In 1965 the Court heard the Corn Exchange Benevolent Society had decided to suspend the service due to insufficient support from its own members. The decline of many family corn merchants in the mid-1960s may have affected the Society's ability to maintain the tradition. The following year the Revd. Cyril Cresswell resigned his position due to ill health and was succeeded by the Revd. Dr. Brian Kirk-Duncan. In 1975 he was appointed Clerk and, as it was felt that he should not hold both appointments, he resigned as Chaplain. Since that time it has been the custom of the Company for each year's Master to choose his own Chaplain for his year in office. Despite these changes the Company has upheld the religious traditions of the City Livery Companies. Attendance at the City's annual United Guild Service at St Paul's Cathedral, a tradition inaugurated in 1943 to raise war-time spirits, has been a regular occasion for collective worship. Since the completion of its own hall in 1987 the Company has conducted its harvest festival, timed to coincide with the yearly installation of the Master, at the venerable medieval church of St Bartholomew the Great, Smithfield, within steps of its Hall. Each year the Master makes a ceremonial offering of a basket of fruit and vegetables.

Just as important for the City livery companies was the yearly round of feasts and ceremonies which punctuated the civic calendar. These solemn occasions were times of elaborate displays, processions and rituals that helped to promote corporate solidarity and to cement relations between the City and the outside world. Lord Mayors have long acted as the official hosts to foreign dignitaries and the City has provided a warm welcome to visitors from afar. The Farmers' Company has since its inception sought modestly to fulfil this role. The annual Livery Dinner, instituted in 1953, provided an annual occasion for hospitality to eminent guests from such as representatives of the Ministry of Agriculture, the National Farmers' Union, the Country Landowners' Association and the Farmers' Club. The 1957 Livery Dinner,

11   Annual Dinner, 1957, from the *Farmer & Stock-Breeder.*

attended amongst others by the Lord Chancellor Viscount Kilmuir and the former Minister of Agriculture Tom Williams, M.P., was a particularly glittering affair. Invitations to guests representing the Nuffield Foundation and the P. & O. Steamship Company helped to re-enforce the Company's plans for travelling bursaries. An important aspect of these events were the after-dinner speeches which gave the opportunity for views to be expressed on the place of agriculture in the nation and the wider world, but without political bias.

Ceremonial insignia and other gifts to the Company

In its early years, while struggling to achieve recognition by the City, the Company began to acquire the physical symbols of livery status. Since the middle ages ceremonial objects such as silver maces, livery gowns, banners and badges had given tangible form to the collective endeavours of the Livery Companies. It was only natural that a new Company, with few roots in the City, should seek to acquire the icons of guild membership. The Company had received a grant of armorial bearings, see colour plate I, from the Earl Marshal as early as 1948 and from that date the Court set about obtaining the whole impedimenta of a London Livery Company.

After several years of delay caused by uncertainties over the liabilities of purchase tax in 1954 the Master, Lord Courthope, presented, at his own cost, a silver ceremonial mace (see p.8), of the short defensive type, made by the master silversmith Francis Cooper. About the same time Lord Courthope investigated the choice of Company's ceremonial colours. After discussion with Lancaster Herald it was decided to adopt gold 'for ripe corn' and burnt sienna 'for the fertile earth'. Ceremonial gowns, to be worn by officers of the Company at all important events, were acquired in 1952.* Three 18-carat gold badges with enamelling, depicting the Company's coat of arms, designed with advice from the College of Arms, were commissioned for use by the Master and Wardens in 1955. At the same time the custom of presenting a badge to Past Masters of the Company was adopted on the retirement of Lord Courthope in 1956. His crucial role in the Company's infancy was marked by the special presentation of a platinum wrist watch.

Gifts by members of the Court of the Company, such as the generous gift of Lord Courthope, became the norm. By tradition the Master of the Company would give a gift to mark the end of his year in office. In 1957 Past Master William Cumber presented a wooden charity box in the form of an old Berkshire dray decorated with imitation sacks of grain, an appropriate gift from a leading light of Berkshire agriculture. Around the same time the Deputy Clerk, Oliver Sunderland, made a gift of a wooden gavel made from oak salvaged from timbers of the blitzed roof of the Guildhall. In 1958 Lance Willet, a West Country farmer and grain importer who was a member of the Baltic Exchange, paid for the installation of the Company's Coat of Arms in the Baltic Exchange.* This was totally devastated by an IRA bomb in 1993 and, though no decision has been reached yet about the future of the building, it is hoped that the window will be replaced when and if the Exchange is eventually

---

* In June 1970 the then Master, Roy Whitwell complained that, having attended several functions in warm weather, his gown was 'something of a burden'. Subsequently a lightweight summer gown for the Master was acquired, in the Company's colours.

* It is understood there is no intention of rebuilding the Exchange as it was.

12 Charity box in the form of an old Berkshire dray with imitation sacks of corn, one of the sacks is provided with a slot designed for a silver collection. Presented by Past Master, William Cumber, C.B.E., in 1957. The charity box was enlarged in 1991.

rebuilt. In June 1973 the Company was lucky enough to win a ballot for placing one of 30 stained glass windows in the West Crypt of Guildhall. Past Master Ronald Borner commemorated his year in office with the gift of an elaborate stained glass window in the West Crypt of the Guildhall (see colour plate IV). Designed by Brian Thomas, a distinguished member of the Glaziers' Company, to a theme planned by Past Master Herbert Graves, the window depicted the history and objectives of the Company. The head of the window contains emblems to indicate the Company's origins in the Red Cross Agricultural Fund.

Perhaps most glorious of all was the gift of the Master's Chain (see colour plate II), presented by Past Master Herbert Graves to commemorate his year in office 1968-69. This sumptuous object was designed around scenes suggested by members of the Court of Assistants and was thus, in Herbert Graves' words, 'a corporate effort'. It consisted of 27 hall-marked silver and heavily gilt links. The centre link consisted of a circular, heavily chased wreath link surmounted by a hand pierced City of London Coat of Arms. The remaining 26 links comprise scallop-shaped links each surmounted by a circular hand enamel painting illustrating the progress and history of British agriculture. The links on either side of the City Arms commemorate the circumstances leading to the formation of the Company. On the right is shown a Spitfire shooting down a Heinkel over the fields of Kent recalling that the war of 1939-45 led those interested in agriculture to work so hard to raise £8,500,000 for the Red Cross Agriculture Fund. On the left are the oak trees planted in Windsor Great Park. The next theme is recorded in the links taken from the 14th-century Luttrell Psalter. Then come three links showing traditional farming occupations: the shepherd with his flock, hand milking—the dairy maid is a member of the 1939 Women's Land Army—and ploughing with shire horses. The fourth theme has three links showing scientific contributions to farming: the plant breeder, the veterinarian and the agricultural merchant delivering scientifically formulated feeds.

13-16   Four silver Loving Cups. *Above left.*
Presented by Liveryman, Willie Emmott, to
commemorate the Grant of Livery, 10 June
1952. *Above right.* In the pattern of a
Porringer and designed in the reign of
Charles II (1686). The original is in the
Ashmolean Museum, Oxford. Presented by
Past Masters Sir Thomas Neame, V.M.H.,
1958-59, and Clare Hawkes, C.B.E. 1959-60.
Below right. Reproduction of George III with
strap motifs. Presented by Past Master Lord
Cromwell, 1960-61. *Left.* Bequeathed in
1962 by Past Master, Nevill Matthews,
M.B.E.

17-19 *Above.* A three-handled Loving Cup surmounted by a fully modelled bull. Presented by Past Master Edward Hitchcock 1967-8. *Above right.* Two Britannia silver Porringers with covers, 1916. Each porringer bears the coat of arms of one of the presenters: Liveryman G.C.H. Matthey and Liveryman H.M. Parsons. *Right.* A silver gilt Loving Cup with cover, 1936. Presented by Liverymen, Freemen and Beadle in memory of the late Learned Clerk, Gordon Sunderland, 1947-66.

20 *Left.* A silver Porringer with cover, 1922. Presented by Past Master Stephen Cheveley, O.B.E., 1961-2.

21 *Below left.* 18ct. white gold and yellow gold 'City of London' emblem brooch set with diamonds and synthetic rubies, presented by Mrs. Hessie Graves, for use by the Master's Lady during her year of office.

These are followed by links showing the farmer's life. First a parson blessing crops on Rogation Sunday with the surveyor, the valuer, the National Agricultural Advisory Service, the farm worker, the estate owner, the farmer and the auctioneer in the congregation: second, hunting, shooting and fishing: third, the show ring, the Burke Trophy awarded at the Royal Agricultural Show. The next and longest series of links consists of nine depicting the development of British farming methods between the foundation of the Company in 1946 and the date of the chain 1969. They include lambs feeding from a nursette, cows in a herringbone parlour, irrigation, crop spraying and a combine harvester. The final theme is a single link illustrating a session of the Company's Advanced Farm Business Management Course discussing a graph on a chalk board, with a projection into the future: 'Maximisation of net profit-gross margin versus variable costs'. The chain was completed in 1971. Past Master Graves' gift was from the heart: it was offered mid way through his year 'in remembrance of my year in office which, if the first five months are any token, will be one of the happiest of my life'. The resulting object, worn every year by the Master, is one of the Company's treasures. In September 1972 Past Master Graves' wife, Mrs. Hessie Graves, graciously donated to the Company a 'City of London' brooch given to her by her husband to mark the first ever Ladies Banquet, to be worn each year by the Master's Lady.

contd. on page 53

22-5 *Above left*. St Paul's Cathedral Solid Silver Royal Wedding Goblet, stem and foot overlaid with pure gold. Presented by Past Master Geoffrey Metson, O.B.E., 1980-1. *Top right*. Three Goblets for the Master (silver gilt) and for the Wardens (silver). Presented by Past Master Victor Parker, M.B.E., 1954-5. *Above left*. Goblet for the Immediate Past Master, in sterling silver Jacobean design in James I period style. Plain polished bowl, gilded inside with baluster knop stem. Bowl engraved with crest of the Company. Foot inscribed 'Immediate Past Master'. Presented by John Borner, Master 1995-6. *Above right*. Eighteen-Carat Gold Goblet commemorating the Investiture of HRH Prince Charles as Prince of Wales, 1 July 1969. Presented by Past Master William Balch, 1970-1.

26 *Far Left.* Sterling Silver Goblet, 1975. Presented by Past Master Leslie Barker, 1974-5. *Right.* Sterling Silver Goblet, 1976, on the occasion of the Clothing with the Livery of HRH Princess Anne and Capt. Mark Phillips. Presented by Past Master Attfield Brooks, O.B.E., T.D., D.L., 1975-6.

27 Four Georgian Silver Salt Cellars and Spoons. Presented by Liveryman John Purbrick, 1951.

28-30 *Above left*. A Sterling Silver 12 in. Salver. Presented by students of the Farm Business Management Course at Folkestone, 1969. *Above right*. A Silver Salver known as the 'Livery Award'. Presented by Past Master Derek Pearce, 1985-6. *Below*. Silver Rose Water Dish, 1966. Presented by Past Master Peter Taylor, T.D., J.P., D.L., 1965-6.

31 *Above.* A pair of Silver Candelabra. Presented by Liveryman Willie Emmott, 1952.

32 *Left.* A pair of Sterling Silver 12 in. Candlesticks, 1938. Bequeathed by Liveryman J.S. Alban-Davies, 1972.

33   A Victorian Silver Gilt Centrepiece with Three Stags at the base, 1848. Presented by Past Master Lord Swaythling, O.B.E., 1962-3.

34 A handwrought chased and embossed sterling silver-gilt two-handled Cup, 1878. Presented by Past Master Roy Whitwell, J.P., 1969/70.

35 Four Silver Salt Cellars and Two Spoons and a Plated 8 in. Tray, the gift of the Farm Business Management Course, 1965.

36 A circular carved silver-plated Rosewater Bowl [measuring] 17½ ins. diameter, made by Elkinton in 1870 and called the 'The Four Elements', similar to the plate presented to the Ladies Champion at Wimbledon. Presented by Past Master Christopher Pertwee, D.L., 1999.

37 An antique sterling silver two-handled Loving Cup and cover in the George II style, made in London in 1899 by Charles Stuart Harris. Presented by Past Master John Cossins, C.B.E., D.L.

These were just a few of the early gifts of regalia by members to the Company. Gifts of silver plate were another tradition of corporate life that early members of the Company readily adopted. In June 1951 John Purbrick proposed to give Georgian silver salt cellars and spoons when the Company obtained its Grant Livery from the City. Though the latter was delayed, Purbrick went ahead with his gift and this marked the initiation of an outpouring of generosity by members. In all, over eight silver loving cups, six silver goblets and one gold, four silver porringers plus three silver salvers, a pair of candlesticks and a Victorian silver gilt centrepiece, a silver candelabra and a silver rose water bowl were given to the Company over the next 40 years. The accompanying photographs to this volume attest to this rich legacy.*

The Earl of Lonsdale's gift

Though it would be invidious to single out any one of the donations of plate, the story of the generous gift of an antique silver flagon and tankard by the Earl of Lonsdale deserves special mention because its fate was bound up with the subsequent history of the Company. In summer 1976 Lord Lonsdale, who had served as Master in 1973-74, proposed a gift of a rare silver flagon and accompanying silver tankard. The two pieces of silver, which had been part of the family collection since the 17th century but had been on loan to the Victoria & Albert Museum, were of unique historic interest. The flagon commemorated the services rendered by Edmund Berry Godfrey, a Justice of the Peace for Westminster during the plague of 1665 and the Great Fire of 1666:

> The gift of Sir Edmund Berry Godfrey, an active and upright magistrate, who, after having rendered valuable service in checking the progress of the plague, received from Charles with the consent of the Privy Council, a silver flagon to commemorate the memory of his patriotic efforts … a man truly born for his country.

The flagon was the gift of Charles II to Godfrey for his services, while the tankard was one of seven given by Godfrey to his friends. Godfrey had an eventful life. In 1678 he was the presiding magistrate who heard the deposition of the adventurer Titus Oates who alleged a 'Popish Plot' existed for the assassination of Charles II and the overthrow of Protestantism. Shortly after hearing Oates' evidence Godfrey was found dead in a ditch on Primrose Hill, 'faced downwards, transfixed by his own sword'. The mystery of his murder, which was never solved, added to the religious and political tensions of the day.

The generous proposal took several years to fulfil, due to delays caused by negotiations with the Inland Revenue as to whether the gift would attract Capital

---

* In 2001, to mark the Company's Jubilee and the Jubilee of Her Majesty the Queen in 2002, an antique sterling silver two-handled Trophy Cup, depicting a chased agricultural scene with scroll leaf handles, hallmarked London 1859, was purchased from a generous donation by Liveryman Ian Whitburn.

38 Tankard.

39 Flagon.

Transfer Tax and liability for insurance. In 1979 Lord Lonsdale made the further generous offer to cover the cost of insurance during his lifetime, in return for the Company undertaking to meet the expense thereafter. He explained his reasons for his generosity in a letter to the Company sent in July : 'I have always thought that these items could never again be used by myself and my descendants because they are so important and would always have to be in a museum.' Lord Lonsdale felt that because of his membership of the Company and the fact that the silver came from the City of London and depicted events in its history that 'a worthy resting place for these items of historic interest would be the Worshipful Company of Farmers'. He added, 'I take that as a Charity, the Worshipful Company of Farmers could never dispose of them except in the event of the Company ceasing to exist. I should be grateful for your assurance on this point'. He recommended that should the Company find the costs of insuring the items after his death too onerous that the Company lend the silver to The Victoria & Albert Museum. In reply the Company promised that the silver 'would not be parted with unless there is a winding-up of the Company' and this provision was duly included in the terms of the gift.

By the mid-1980s the costs of the Hall threatened the Company's ability to support the Wye College courses. As a result the Company requested that Lord Lonsdale alter the terms of his gift to allow them to sell the silver. Some of the Court demurred from this move but Lord Lonsdale agreed and in September 1985 the Company was released from the terms which required the gift to be held in perpetuity.

Proceeds of the sale were to be placed in an educational trust fund, the Lord Lonsdale Trust, the income of which was to be used to fund the Advanced Farm Business Management Course at Wye, or failing that some other aspect of agricultural education. The silver, which was auctioned at Christie's on 27 November 1985, fetched some £95,000.

Good Causes: The Benevolent Fund

In its earliest days the Company's struggle to establish its finances and official status prevented it from supporting good causes in all but the most modest ways. Prior to the Grant of Livery it was felt necessary to husband the Company's resources. Appeals to contribute to the annual Lord Mayor's Appeal in June 1950 were regretfully refused due to insufficient funds. £21 was given to the Lord Mayor's Flood Distress Fund in March 1953 to relieve the distress caused by the recent East Coast floods but further applications for charity were refused 'having regard to the Company's finances'. A further £21 was also given to the King George VI National Memorial Fund. During this period modest investments were being built up. Individual members led by example. In March 1953 the Court of Assistants heard through the Clerk of the Gardeners' Company of the plight of the recently orphaned son, one of four, of an employee of *The City Press* who was anxious to take up farming as a career. Sir Richard Haddon, in a private act of kindness, offered to give the boy 12 months' practical experience prior to his entry into the Surrey Farming Institute. By December 1953 the Company felt able to contribute 25 guineas to the restoration of St Stephen Walbrook, damaged during the Blitz, and the location of the Company's first church service. At the same time a request from the Royal Agricultural Benevolent Institution, the country's largest farming charity, was turned down, according to the Court of Assistants, because of 'the necessity for conserving the funds of the Company, which is a young one'. In recent years the Company has given a substantial sum per year to the RABI.

In the midst of the final negotiations to obtain the Grant of Livery, the Company set about creating a benevolent fund. In June 1954 Claude Pendlebury, M.C., a Devonport-based land agent and Past President of the Chartered Land Agents Society, who had joined the Company in 1948 and had recently been elected onto the Court of Assistants, suggested that thought be given to the idea of creating a benevolent fund, 'however small it might be in the initial phase'. The idea was passed to the General Purposes Committee for consideration and later that year it recommended that an *ad hoc* committee be formed to discuss all matters relating to the proposal, including a draft of Declaration of Trust for making donations to the Fund. At the same time it was agreed that Lt. Col. Norman Letts, senior partner in the City firm of Messrs. Mawby, Barrie and Letts, who had joined the Company in

1950, should be asked to act as Honorary Solicitor to provide legal advice. Further progress was delayed until the Company received its Charter which would enable the Company to have the power to administer trust deeds, and in December 1955 the Court named five of its number, Victor Parker, Sir Cleveland Fyfe, Stephen Cheveley and Nevill Matthews, along with the newly appointed Honorary Chaplain, Cyril Cresswell, as Trustees. Claude Pendlebury, who had first suggested the creation of the Fund, was made Honorary Almoner. In March 1956 a Declaration of Trust formally constituted the Benevolent Fund. Under the terms of the Declaration the purposes of the Fund were to provide for the relief of necessitous members, ex-members, employees, ex-employees or their dependants. At the time of the Declaration of Trust it was reported that 27 members of the Company had entered into seven-year covenants to contribute £188, while a further 11 had promised a yearly donation of £43. At that time it was reported that some £324 had been received in donations. Later that year small grants were made to the City & Guilds Institute and the restoration fund of St Mary le Bow. Later that year the Company responded to appeals by the Lord Mayor on behalf of victims of the Soviet invasion of Hungary and the Anglo-Egyptian Relief Fund to provide for British nationals affected by the Suez Crisis. By December 1960 the Benevolent Fund had grown to some £2,000 and it was decided that collections should be made at the Company's annual church service and at Court Luncheons. Walter Cardy became Honorary Almoner on the death of Claude Pendlebury in September 1961 and began an energetic effort to raise money for the Fund. By March 1962 the Fund had grown by a third and it was hoped that it would amount to £5,000 within 18 months. During this period the Company broadened the scope of its charitable donations, giving support to members' widows, providing a small loan to the son of a deceased member who had come into financial difficulty, donating sums to public charities such as the World Refugee Year Fund, The Royal Agricultural Benevolent Institution's Autumn Days Fund, which was set up to provide assistance to the elderly, and the Lady Hoare Thalidomide Fund. The Benevolent Fund paid out 50 guineas to the 1968 Foot and Mouth Appeal by the NFU while an emergency appeal to the membership, suggested by Past Master Stephen Cheveley, who was a scientific advisor to the Foot and Mouth Institute, raised some £380. The epidemic also forced postponement of the Company's 1968 annual January Livery Dinner and Service to the following May. A good sense of the way in which the charitable aims of the Company were met can be given by the example of the gift of 100 guineas given to the Benevolent Fund by Edward Hitchcock in lieu of a gift of plate, to mark the occasion of the completion of his son's apprenticeship in 1959.

Walter Cardy's time as Honorary Almoner was notable for his attempt to expand the scope of the Company's charitable activities. At a special meeting of the Finance

Committee held in May 1966 he suggested setting up an appeal to the Livery for 10-year interest free loans of £1,000 each. Though the Committee thought the proposal was an excellent idea, some doubts were expressed as to whether the majority of the members would be able to make such loans, 'experience has shown in the past that comparatively few members of the livery would be prepared to contribute' and that such an appeal might have an adverse affect on recruiting new members. Despite these reservations, Almoner Cardy was allowed further to formulate these proposals in the following months. His idea for creating a fund for future projects took shape after his election as Master in September 1966. In December of that year he formally proposed the creation of a fund worth some £17,000 'for furthering the Company's aims and objects and to pass on to future members of the Company a strong financial heritage'. Following discussion by the Court of Assistants, which centred on the use which would be made of the funds raised and the timing of the appeal, the Court agreed in principle to set up a scheme 'to strengthen the funds of the Company'.

Thereafter a series of meetings were held between the Master, the Clerk and the Honorary Solicitor, Geoffrey Metson, who had been appointed when Norman Letts died in September 1966. A Liveryman since 1955, Geoffrey Metson combined a deep interest in agriculture with a long established legal practice in the City; he had been Secretary and later Director General of the National Association of Corn and Agricultural Merchants and kept the pedigree herd of Coverwood Poll Herefords. This group constituting a special sub-committee on finance, which cogitated on a range of ideas for raising funds; interest free loans, deeds of covenant and trusts for the avoidance of death duty. It was considered that various alternative forms should be available to Liverymen in order that they could select those which were most appropriate to their own particular financial circumstances. After taking legal advice the sub-committee decided to recommend that the Company's ordinances and by-laws be altered to allow the Benevolent Fund and the Educational Fund to be re-constituted to enable funds to be transferred from one to the other and to facilitate the further raising of funds from the membership by various means. These proposals were accepted by the Court in June 1967 and at the installation ceremony of the new Master, Edward Hitchcock, the Clerk read out a letter from Senior Past Master Sir Richard Haddon in praise of Walter Cardy's efforts: 'his enthusiasm and his planning for the future I commend … If his plans fructify—and they exceed my wildest dreams when the Company was formed—we shall be in his everlasting debt, as in fact we are for his work over the years'.

Honorary Members

As a mark of respect and as a token of its affection the Company has since its inception bestowed the freedom on individuals. Through this means the Company has formed firm friendships and associations within the City and in the wider world. The first person to be made an Honorary Liveryman was the Revd. Cyril Cresswell, the Chaplain who was proposed as a member in September 1951, an honour which he was later to have said he 'much appreciated'. The Company was particularly eager to demonstrate its appreciation to those who had helped the Company in its early years. The next man to be so honoured was Alec Dodds Robertson, the Secretary to the Red Cross Agricultural Fund 1939-1946. In November 1952 the Master, Lord Courthope, moved a resolution to grant him the Honorary Livery of the Company, as a means of marking 'its cordial appreciation of the devoted and unfailing services rendered'; the Master's resolution was carried unanimously. Other Honorary Liverymen during this period included Alderman Rupert De La Bere (clothed 1953) and The Earl Jowitt, P.C., formerly Minister of Agriculture (clothed 1953). Alderman Sir George Wilkinson, Lord Mayor during the Blitz, who had helped the Company in its pursuit of the Grant of Livery, was elected Honorary Liveryman in September 1957, 'having regard to his signal services to the Company in its early days'. In 1960 Sir Bernard Waley Cohen, the then Lord Mayor, was also elected Honorary Liveryman and over the years attended many Company functions.

In subsequent years the Company has granted honorary membership to a variety of individuals. In 1974 Ian Reid, who had been so crucial to the success of the Company's involvement with Wye College, was granted Honorary Freedom and Livery of the Company. His response to the honour, conveyed to the Company in a letter to the Clerk, fully conveyed the sense of warmth that underlay the formality of the grant. Reid expressed himself 'almost without words' but went on to state, 'you will have no idea of the pleasure and happiness of the good friends and colleagues and the generosity of the Worshipful Company which have come to me since the Folkestone Courses began'.

Since the 15th century the livery companies have forged a relationship with the Crown through honorary membership. Through the centuries members of the royal family have graced the ranks of the Livery Companies. So it was with the Farmers. In March 1975 the Company was delighted to hear from the then Master, Leslie Barker, that HRH Princess Anne had agreed to accept an invitation to become an Honorary Liveryman. The Company was further gratified to hear in June of that year that HRH The Prince of Wales indicated that he too would be willing to be nominated as an Honorary Liveryman of the Company. On 8 June 1976, after an ordinary meeting of the Court of Assistants, HRH Princess Anne (along with Captain Mark Phillips) made the necessary declaration and was elected and clothed. Sadly, the untimely death of Leslie Barker in a car accident on his way from the Advanced Farm Business Management Course at Newcastle prevented

40   Clothing of HRH Princess Anne in 1976 by the Master, Lt. Col. Attfield Brooks, with (from left to right) Past Master Sir Nigel Strutt, Past Master Michael Cheveley, Assistant Trevor Muddiman and the Clerk, the Rev. Brian Kirk Duncan.

41   Presentation of scroll to HRH Prince of Wales by the Master, R.J. Harrison, J.P., with Past Master Stephen Cheveley, Assistant Philip Henman and Assistant Sir Charles Graham.

42 Copy of the scroll presented to HRH Prince of Wales, 1980.

him from witnessing this historic event. It was not until July 1980 that HRH The Prince of Wales, after a Court Luncheon held at Skinners' Hall, was duly elected and clothed.

A 'Godfatherly Interest'

In autumn 1956 the Company began what proved to be a long-standing relationship with the National Federation of Young Farmers' Clubs. The link was first mooted in a letter from Douglas Bird, a Liveryman, to the Junior Warden, Nevill Matthews. The letter reported how during that year's Royal Show he had had a visit from the new General Secretary of the Federation, Major General R. F. Cornwall. General Cornwall had sounded out Bird about the possibility of the Farmers acting as a sponsor to the organisation. According to Bird's letter, when asked what he meant by the use of the word sponsor, the General had replied that what he had in mind was 'somebody to act as a godfather, and take a godfatherly interest in the movement's activities'. When probed further by Bird, General Cornwall suggested a minimal degree of financial support by way of the analogy he had already used: 'when he was asked to act as a godfather he said he would be delighted to do so so long as that parents did not expect him to do more than give say 5/- on his godchild's birthday and at Christmas'. General Cornwall was invited to attend a Court Luncheon in December that year to discuss the matter further. At that meeting General Cornwall made an extensive presentation to the Company of the current state of the NFYFC.

Founded in 1932 as a rural youth movement, the Federation, which had 10,000 members, had just undergone a change of leadership and was facing a substantial deficit. It lacked a Royal Patron and was looking for support from a 'really influential worthwhile body', especially as it was about to celebrate the silver jubilee of its foundation. Major General Cornwall proposed to the Court a 'free association' between the Company and the Federation by which his organisation could benefit from the prestige and status associated with a City Livery Company but also through the 'support, goodwill and specialised and greatly varied advice of the members of the Company'. He added, 'if I may be rather trite and pompous, your Company would gain that sense of reward and satisfaction which can only come from an even fuller discharge of your true functions'. Impressed by his arguments the Court immediately decided to see what it could do.

In early 1957 it was decided that the Company would nominate a representative to the Federation's Executive Council as a co-opted member. In addition the Company undertook to supervise the presentation of illuminated certificates to each Master Craftsman elected by the Federation each year. At the same time it was agreed that the Master would issue an appeal to the membership for donations to the Federation's Jubilee Fund. By these means £290 was raised for the Federation and through the good offices of Sir Patrick Gower, Managing Director of the advertising firm of Charles F. Higham Ltd., some 60 illuminated certificates bearing the Company's arms were procured for presentation.

Thereafter for the next 10 years the Company regularly participated in the awards ceremony to the Federation's Master Craftsmen. Each year the Master would attend the Federation's AGM as the Company's representative. During this period the number of certificates being awarded by the Federation grew. By the mid-1960s, just as the Company's involvement with Wye College was deepening, concerns grew that the number of certificates being issued was debasing the value of the Farm Business Management Awards. In March 1965, one of the moving figures behind the Wye experiment, Past Master Stephen Cheveley, wrote that 'the whole thing is getting rather big and out of hand' and recommended that the Company cease to take part in the Federation's award scheme. Thereafter, with great regret, the Court decided to end the award of the certificates. In 1967 the practice of each year's Master acting as representative on the Federation's Executive Council was altered and from then on, in order to ensure continuity, it was decided to appoint a representative. The immediate Past Master Walter Cardy agreed to act in this capacity and did so for several years after which his place was taken by Past Master Frank Garner. A senior member of the Company has regularly represented the Company on the Council of the NFYFC and Company members have been prominent in the Young Farmers movement including past National Presidents HRH Princess Anne (1974-1976, 1991-1993), Sir Henry

43 The Worshipful Company of Farmers' Challenge Cup. 6½ in. solid silver cup, hallmarked Birmingham 1927. Presented by Past Master Roy Whitwell, 1977.

Plumb (1976-1986) and Sir Richard Butler (1993-1997). Young Farmers are eligible for the Henman travel grants and regularly form about a quarter of all those receiving the grants. In 1977 a silver cup was donated by Past Master Roy Whitwell to be given in the Company's name to the Young Farmers as part of the Federation's annual counties competition. Since that time the Worshipful Company of Farmers Trophy, as the cup is officially known, has been awarded to the champion small county federation in national competition finals whose membership is under 800. Sadly, because of a shrinking membership, most counties now have 800 members or less. It was therefore decided that the Trophy was to be awarded to the champion small county whose membership figures are amongst the lowest 50 per cent of counties.

During the 1960s the membership of the Company gradually began to alter. The older generation who had founded the Company began to make way for a new generation of men who had joined the Company after the Grant of Livery. Senior Past Masters Nevill Matthews, Sir Patrick Gower, Sir Cleveland Fyfe and Sir Richard Haddon, as well as the able Clerk Oliver Gordon Sunderland, who had all worked so hard to set up the Company, all passed away during this period. Stalwart members such as Sir Thomas Neame, Victor Parker, and Lord Swaythling continued to do sterling service, and veteran members such as Stephen Cheveley and Walter Cardy were to take a leading role in taking the Company in new directions in the years to come. But their efforts were to be augmented by the addition of a cohort of slightly younger men who helped to see the Company through the period of the establishment of the Folkestone courses and the changes in the Company's Benevolent Fund. This group included Frank Garner, Leslie Barker, The Rt. Hon. the Earl of Lonsdale, William Balch and Ronald Borner, who were all elected to the Court of Assistants in December 1964. Philip Henman, who provided generous financial assistance to the Company, along with much appreciated advice and assistance with regard to investments and property, was co-opted on to the Court at the same time.

By the early 1960s the size of the Company's Livery was nearing the limit of 250 set down in its Charter. In 1961 in was necessary to set up a waiting list for freemen eligible for clothing in the Livery. By March 1963 there were some 245 Liverymen, 93 Freemen and some 16 apprentices. An option was to petition the Court of Aldermen for an increase in the size of the Livery. This would allow admission to the livery of all those men on the waiting list, including a number of 'eminent and substantial persons' according to the Company's subsequent petition, as well as providing additional funding which, the Clerk asserted, 'the Company would undoubtedly need in the future'. The Court readily agreed to this and in early 1965 a petition was presented to the Court of Aldermen through the good offices of Liveryman and Alderman Sir Ralph Perring. On 18 May 1965 the Court of Aldermen agreed to the prayer of the petition. The Company's request is indicative of an increasing sense of the Company's place in the City. At the same time that the Company was appealing for the increase in the size of the Livery, it was making it known to a group of representatives of the National Dairy Council that it would oppose an attempt to set up a separate Dairymen's Guild.

The increased size of the Livery attested to the vigour of the Company's membership, but it posed its own dilemma. The more men who joined the Company, the greater the need for an appropriate venue for Company meetings. From its earliest days the Company had been peripatetic, relying on the good offices of various persons and institutions for places to meet. As has been seen, from 1947 to 1950 it met at the Café Royal. A meeting of the General Purposes Committee in March 1951 at Innholders' Hall in College Street marked the Company's first formal meeting within the boundaries of the Square Mile and for the next three decades Innholders' Hall was to be a regular venue for meetings of the Court and the General Purposes Committee. Smaller meetings, to discuss matters such as the travelling bursaries scheme, were held at the offices of the Clerk, Gordon Sunderland, at 15 Eastcheap. Meetings of the Court were also held at Tallow Chandlers' Hall, Fishmongers' Hall, the Guildhall, Trinity House, Tower Hill, Goldsmiths' Hall, Painter Stainers' Hall and Ironmongers' Hall. A special meeting of the Court of Assistants to discuss the arrangements for the Folkestone courses was held in July 1962 at the offices of Walter Cardy, in Tilney Street, W1. About this time the Company received a circular from the Chamberlain's Court of the City which would point to an issue which would dominate the Company's affairs for years to come. The powerful General Purposes Committee of the Court of Aldermen had instructed the Chamberlain to write to the Livery Companies to suggest that all the administrative meetings of the Companies should always be held in the City. The Company had fought hard for its status as a City Livery Company, but without a formal place of meeting it would always be dependent on the availability of meeting places and the goodwill of others. To many in the Company a solution had to be found. The long search for a home in the City forms the subject of the next chapter in the Company's history.

Chapter Five

THE HALL PROJECT

Introduction: 'The first new hall built in the city for over 200 years'

In the early 1960s the Company embarked on what was to prove a long and arduous search for a permanent home in the City of London. This was a task which was to call upon all the resources and expertise that the Company could muster. The acquisition of a site for a hall and its ultimate construction took place over some 20 years, a period which witnessed dramatic swings in the commercial property market, changes in planning policy and a growing concern with the conservation of the built environment. All these factors were to present difficulties to the Company. Despite these, the Company, in conjunction with the Worshipful Company of Fletchers, was ultimately to be successful in undertaking what was to be a unique venture: the first newly-built Livery Hall to be constructed in the City of London for more than two centuries.

In ancient times, when the guilds were first founded they tended to meet in the houses of their members. From the 14th century, as their status and wealth accumulated, the guilds, through gifts and endowments of members, began to purchase property in the City of London. Often this consisted of mansion houses belonging to noblemen but eventually some of the Companies began to construct their own purpose-built halls. Stoutly constructed in stone and lavishly decorated with Arras tapestries, stone carvings and stained glass, these buildings formed the focus for the corporate life of the Livery Companies. They provided the venue for the great occasions of state, the lavish feasts and ceremonial meetings which characterised the guilds of the middle ages. They also served for the storage of ancient muniments and silver plate and acted as the site for the day-to-day administration of guild life—the signing of apprenticeship indentures, the enrolling of new members, the administration of property and the dispensing of charity.

Over the centuries, as the role of the livery companies changed, many of these buildings were rebuilt and, in some cases, sold off. The Great Fire of London of 1666 destroyed some 44 Livery Halls. Many of these were rebuilt in the lavish style of the Restoration. New Livery Companies were founded in the later 17th century and these also built new halls. The Gunmakers' Hall in Whitechapel, constructed in 1757, was the last hall to be newly built (as opposed to rebuilt) before the 20th century. In the intervening period many of the smaller Livery Companies, whose fortunes were linked to their right to regulate the crafts of the City of London, became defunct and their halls were sold off and demolished. The blitz of 1940-41 took a heavy toll, destroying or damaging over 25 of these ancient edifices. In the post-war years the older Livery Companies, through a judicious mixture of income from war damage compensation payments and property development, managed to rebuild. The need to defray the costs of construction of these new halls meant that these building projects had to include a significant commercial element. The result was a new type of livery hall, surmounted by income-generating offices. The future Farmers' Hall as it was to be realised conformed to this new tradition.

In its early years other pressing concerns of the Company, especially the negotiations with the City Corporation over the Grant of Livery and the setting up of the various early educational schemes, meant that it had passed up the opportunity of acquiring a hall. In March 1951 the Master, Lord Courthope, told a General Purposes Committee that he had had a conversation with Past Lord Mayor Alderman Sir George Wilkinson who had previously advised the Company on its petition for a Grant of Livery. Sir George had offered the Company a hall, together with offices, in Blackfriars which was available for a rental of £3,000 per annum. The matter was discussed, but 'having regard to the present financial condition of the Company and to the commitments which the Court visualised in connection with certain of their objects', the offer was declined, 'much as it was appreciated'. No more formal consideration was given to acquiring a hall for more than a decade.

The impetus for the acquisition of a hall appears to have originated with Walter Cardy, who as Junior Warden and later as Master had done so much to widen the scope of the Company's benevolent fund. The first indication that the Company was interested in acquiring a hall came in December 1963 when Walter Cardy suggested that the Company should consider 'providing a capital structure which will enable the Company to broaden its activities and to provide itself with a hall forming part of a commercial building which will provide revenue for the Company in years to come. The suggestion was taken up and in September 1964 the General Purposes Committee of the Company was informed by the Clerk of enquiries which he had made about a piece of freehold land near Cannon Street which Junior Warden Cardy had told him would shortly be up for sale. Having received the particulars Cardy had, however, come to the conclusion that the property was 'far beyond the scope of the Company' but added that he was making enquiries about other suitable sites. The original plan the Company had envisaged was the building of an income-producing office block containing a Livery Hall, along the lines of other post-war rebuilding of Livery Company Halls. This was to be financed out of interest-free loans from Company members repayable out of income received from the letting of offices.

The search for an appropriate site was to prove an arduous task. Junior Warden Cardy warned the Court of Assistants 'that finding a freehold site was not an easy matter, and it may take a long time to do so'. At the same time Alderman Sir Ralph Perring said that it was a custom of London that the Hall should be situate within the City boundaries. This was the point (June 1964) at which the Company was told of the City Corporation's circular which had declared that all administrative meetings of the Livery should, if possible, be held in the square mile. Despite the apparent difficulties of finding a site Cardy embarked on an extensive search for property for the Company. His initial enquiries led him to take advice from Sir Ralph Perring who recommended him to get in touch with Mr. Fox of Messrs. W.B. Hallett, Fox and White which he had done. Mr. Fox had expressed great keenness to help and told him that he would let Mr. Cardy know if he found anything suitable. After more than six months' search Cardy was unable to report any progress. This was an inauspicious point at which to consider engaging in building an office block. The government of Harold Wilson, which was elected in March 1964, passed new legislation which strictly controlled, through a system of permits, the construction of new offices, the so-called 'Brown Ban', after the Labour minister George Brown, who had devised the legislation. Because of these restrictions the Company's search for a site was apparently stymied. Junior Warden Cardy told the General Purposes Committee in March 1965 that there was 'no prospect at the present time of the scheme getting off the ground', though he undertook to watch for opportunities which might occur to acquire a freehold.

For almost a year Walter Cardy continued to search for a suitable site, viewing some six properties, all of which were found wanting. In his year as Master he continued the search with vigour, but to no avail. In March 1967 he attempted to take the matter further. He had been in touch with Mr. Bernard Thorpe, Immediate Past Master of the Gold and Silver Wyre Drawers' Company, who was considering the possibility of building a joint office block and livery hall in conjunction with other livery companies. So far other companies had shown interest. The Master, Walter Cardy, had given particulars to Mr. Thorpe of a site he had found the previous year which at the time he considered had been too big for the Farmers' Company to finance alone. When told of this possible collaboration with other Livery Companies, it was reported that all the members of the Court 'consider it desirable that this matter should be keenly pursued'.

Despite this fulsome endorsement no further action was taken for another two years. Then, in the year of office of Herbert Graves as Master, 1968-1969, the first

I   The Grant of Arms

II   The Master's Chain

III   The Master's Chair

IV   The Stained Glass Window

concrete steps towards the eventual realisation of a hall began to be taken. The role of Herbert Graves in the Hall project deserves special mention. A Liveryman since 1953, Herbert Graves was a Lloyd's underwriter and partner of a merchant banking firm which floated the 'Bemax' firm of Vitamins, famous among farmers for its 'Vitamealo' feeding stuffs. He later succeeded Walter Cardy as the moving spirit in the scheme and presided over the committee to oversee the project which was constituted in his year as Master from its inception to the start of negotiations with the Fletchers' Company, a period of service of 14 years during which he dictated hundreds of letters.

In June 1969 Herbert Graves sought to push forward Walter Cardy's hopes for a Hall. He circulated a memorandum to the Court of Assistants which he had sent to Walter Cardy about the present situation. According to his memo the scheme of the Gold and Silver Wyre Drawers had failed to get off the ground. There was, however 'still the keenest possible interest' in the possibility of building a joint Hall between several companies. Graves' open memo acknowledged the difficulties: 'It is', he wrote, 'obviously necessary to keep one's objectives within the limits of financial feasibility and in this connection we are all handicapped today in a way that did not arise, say, 800 years ago'. The greatest difficulty was, according to him, 'the fantastic price of freehold land in the City of London'. In his memo the Master outlined in embryo the financial basis for building a Hall: 'I find—on current enquiry—that a Worthy Hall—with ancillary accommodation, capable of being let at rentals to amortise the total cost of the Hall within a few decades, could be built and equipped today for a sum in the neighbourhood of £250,000'. Graves envisaged a scheme by which some five or six Livery Companies would club together, each investing between £40,000 and £50,000 to purchase a site and build and equip a Hall for joint use. The building would consist of a Hall with an office block above which it was hoped would produce a rental income which would eventually amortise the cost of the project.

The Master referred to a recent visit he had paid to the newly-rebuilt Barber Surgeons' Hall, 'a really remarkably beautiful and suitable building for the purpose' which he was told was producing rental income which would pay for the cost of the building over a 40-year period. Graves strongly recommended to the Court meeting that the Company pursue this sort of venture, in collaboration with others. After discussion of his memo the Court decided that the Company should try to build a Hall on its own. At the same time the Company's search was put on a formal footing. A small sub-committee—the nucleus of the later Hall Management Committee— was formed, consisting of Past Master Walter Cardy, the Honorary Chaplain Brian Kirk Duncan and the Master, Herbert Graves, who was to continue after his year in office. Thus constituted, the small sub-committee set about its task with vigour.

'A Gentlemen's Agreement'

In September 1969 the sub-committee heard word, through Mr. Charles Wilson of the well known City firm of Chamberlain and Willows, of a small freehold site near Smithfield Market owned by the University of Durham. The site consisted of 1,500 square feet comprising two small late Victorian warehouses, approximately 50 yards from the newly reopened Barbican underground station, located in an area designated by the Corporation of London as a redevelopment zone. The University was asking for between £15-16,000 for the site, 22-23 Newbury Street and 10-11 Middle Street.

The opportunity seemed to the Company too good to pass up and in early February 1970 a special meeting of the General Purposes Committee was called to consider all the options in regard to purchase of the site. The building had been inspected by the sub-committee who reported that they 'felt it was an excellent opportunity to gain a freehold in the city and, eventually, own hall'. Past Master Geoffrey Parsons and Philip Henman endorsed this view. Herbert Graves had consulted a firm of architects, Michael Rayner and Partners, who had produced an informal estimate of £120,000 for building a hall and offices. It was envisaged that, because of its location in a development zone, it would be necessary to put the site in 'cold storage' for six or seven years, until the City Corporation developed the land in the vicinity, when it was possible that the Corporation of London might offer an alternative site, or, as the Special Committee minutes put it, 'in other words the Company was acquiring a foothold near the place where it would eventually be possible to build a hall'. The University of Durham were said to be 'keen to get their money now, rather than await the Corporation's re-development scheme'.

At the special meeting it was soon realised that the site itself was too small for a Hall and that it would be necessary to purchase the adjoining property. Charles Wilson had said that he could acquire an option on the adjoining plot which would give the Company some 4,000 square feet. Assistant William Balch, a chartered surveyor who had joined the Company in 1956 and who was later to provide much useful advice, expressed the view that 'the site was good and it would be wise to get a foot in the door'. The plot was, according to him, 'cheap' and if the Company desired eventually to build a Hall they should buy this plot now and then be in a strong position to negotiate with the Corporation of London. Alternatively, if negotiations with the City Corporation did not proceed on a favourable basis, 'there would be little lost, as he felt that after two years' time the plot could be sold, possibly without loss'. It was agreed that Wilson should notify the surveyor acting for the University, Mr. G.W. Towse, that a firm decision would be made in the middle of March and he would ask them if they would keep 'a gentleman's agreement' until that date, that is, notifying them if another prospective purchaser appeared on the scene. The meeting of the General Purposes Committee recommended purchase to the Court of Assistants and voted to support Past Master Graves and the other members of the sub-committee in any action they had to take 'if the position became difficult' before the Court met in mid-March.

This was perhaps a premonition of the problems to come. Two weeks before the Court met, on 3 March 1970, the University's surveyor telephoned Charles Wilson with news that one of the leaseholders, an umbrella manufacturer, Messrs. Swaine, Adeney, Brigg & Sons Ltd. of Piccadilly, who had earlier been interested in acquiring the freehold, had contacted Towse to offer to better the Company's initial offer of £15,250 by several hundred pounds. Mr. Towse said he was 'in a very embarrassing position in view of the assurances he had previously given us but had to recognise his duty to the University'. This news did not represent any great difficulty but it was realised that since Messrs. Swaine, Adeney, Brigg & Sons were in the process of vacating the building and offering their own lease for sale there was a strong possibility that there was another purchaser, lurking, as Charles Wilson put it, 'on the scene' to acquire the site. Wilson acted quickly, verbally assuring Durham's surveyor that he would strongly recommend that the Company meet this higher price. In the light of this it was decided by the Court of Assistants on 17 March to go ahead with the purchase with a revised offer of £16,000. The initial purchase was financed by the hall's prime mover, Past Master Walter Cardy.

Before the formalities of the purchase had been agreed Durham's surveyor telephoned Wilson once again with more unwelcome news. The property firm of Jones, Lang and Wootten, acting on behalf of the developers Laing, had attempted to 'gazump' the Company by offering £4,500 more for the site. This higher offer placed the representatives of The University of Durham in a very difficult position. While the University wanted to keep to the gentlemen's agreement to sell the property to the Farmers, it had a duty of trust to look after its own interests. Fortunately for the Company, Mr. Towse was, as Herbert Graves described him, 'a man of honour'.

An urgent meeting was arranged by Charles Wilson with Mr. Towse and members of the Hall Committee. The University's surveyor expressed regret and embarrassment at the situation, but, after explaining the University's Trustees' obligations to their institution, asked if the Company could see its way to increasing its offer. It was then decided that the Company would agree to make a £2,000 donation to the University's general fund, to be spread over four years. In addition to this, Walter Cardy and Philip Henman promised a further £1,000 each in recognition of Durham's adherence to the original 'gentlemen's agreement'. The agreement between the University and the Company was based on the understanding that the site would only ever be developed as a Livery Hall. Of the high principles that seemed to govern the negotiations Walter Cardy later commented: 'the decision of the University is I think in accordance with the tradition one would expect of an organisation of their standing. Having said that one recognises the courage required to adhere to their bargain. I confess it is good to know that such standards still exist'. As a result of this agreement the University's property was purchased by the Company's Charitable Trust, a modest freehold site near historic Smithfield Market, with sitting tenants with leases of seven years to run.

Negotiations with Developers and Planning Consent

Thus by June 1970 the Company had made the first halting steps towards the acquisition of a Hall. At the time members of the Court began to be aware of the potential for difficulties which lay ahead. Past Master Geoffrey Parsons gave warning that 'we must look for a long period of complexity and possibly trouble'. Though the Company was ultimately to attain its goal of a Hall this warning was to prove all too true.

Once the Durham University site had been purchased the Company quickly set about trying to purchase the adjoining freehold, 19-21 Newbury Street and 12-14 Middle Street, owned by the Ellerman Shipping Line. The acquisition of the adjoining site took several years, dogged by the doubts over the Corporation's plans for the area, the difficulties of finding a potential developer, and the uncertainties of the property market. In 1970 the restrictions on office development were lifted and a development boom ensued. According to Herbert Graves, though it was extremely difficult to put a proper value on the property, it was not unrealistic to suppose that in the light of present circumstances the site price could be as much as £750,000 by mid-1976. In that year the small sub-committee was reconstituted as the Hall (Property Management) Committee to include the then Master, Ronald Borner, the Honorary Solicitor, Geoffrey Metson, and Alderman Michael Hinton. William Balch was later co-opted onto the Hall Committee. The prospects of building a Hall were buoyed up by the boom in the property market. This came to an abrupt end in 1974 after the onset of world-wide recession. In March 1974 the new Labour government imposed a Development Tax and a near total ban on grants of Office Development Permits. High interest rates further dampened the property market. During this period the Company sought out potential collaborating developers, including Laing, who had earlier attempted to 'gazump' the Company. These came to nothing. A verbal 'deal' with another developer was arranged by Chamberlain and Willows in 1973 but this collapsed before completion in the economic crisis of 1974. The adjacent property, 19-21 Newbury Street and 12-14 Middle Street, was finally acquired by the Company in 1976 for £110,000. This was paid for by a Hall Appeal Fund set up by the Master, Lt. Col. Attfield Brooks. Donations, interest free loans and covenants from some 70 Liverymen and five Freemen raised £50, 000. The remainder was raised by a loan from the Company's Corporate Body plus generous assistance from several individual Liverymen, including Sir John Eastwood, a Nottinghamshire-based farmer and civil engineering contractor, who gave £35,000. Walter Cardy, the prime mover of the Hall project, again demonstrated his generosity by providing an interest free loan of £9,000. This was one of his last acts on behalf of the Company; it was with great sadness that the Company learned of his death in October 1976.

Once the adjoining site was purchased the Hall Committee set about finding a developer as well as dealing with the tenants. Vacant possession at the end of leases often proved difficult to obtain; on one occasion it was thought necessary for the City of London Police to be in attendance when bailiffs attempted to take possession, though no violence occurred. The property market remained depressed but in September 1978 the Company began negotiations with Imry Property Holdings Ltd. The terms of the deal with Imry looked promising. In return for undertaking the construction of a Hall and adjacent offices Imry would be granted a 125-year lease, paying £8,000 per annum rent from December 1978 rising to £18,000 on completion of the building or 25 per cent of rental income, whichever was the greater. All this was subject to planning permission being granted by the City Corporation, a responsibility which was vested in the developer to obtain. This proved a significant stumbling block.

Public attitudes to office development underwent dramatic change in the 1970s. The publication in 1976 of the *Save Our City* report by The Society for the Protection of Ancient Buildings, the Georgian Group and the Victorian Society began to challenge the wisdom of comprehensive redevelopment in favour of a policy of conservation. The City Corporation's plans for redevelopment of the area of Smithfield in which the hall site was located were substantially affected by the publication of a new Smithfield District Plan in 1978 which placed greater emphasis on retaining the 19th-century street-scape, and small-scale workshop industries which characterised the area around Smithfield Market. Originally designated as a site for office block development the Company's site was now considered to be in a conservation area. The Farmers' planning application, drawn up by the architects Norman Levinson and Partners, was submitted in September 1978 to the Corporation's Architecture and Planning Department and this was initially found to be acceptable, subject to minor modifications on aesthetic grounds. But after a campaign for the conservation of the site was launched, officers of the Town Planning Department began to question the Company's proposals. A Committee for the Conservation of Middle Street was formed by tenants and local residents which was supported by conservation groups and persons of note, including the Poet Laureate, Sir John Betjeman, who had lived in nearby Cloth Fair. Petitions to the Corporation, a small public demonstration and an unfavourable mention in the 'Peterborough' column in *The Daily Telegraph* and in *The City Press* were among the manifestations of opposition to the Company's proposals. In July 1979 the Planning Department advised the Company of 'considerable public reaction to the scheme' and, after some delay, further advised in October 1979 that the application had 'generated much local interest as the scheme involves loss of buildings whose scale and design are important to the character of the area' as well as a loss of premises for the small businesses which used the site.

Fortunately for the Company the attitude of central government towards granting consent to such schemes was changing. Ministerial Circular 61/53 from the Department of the Environment issued in October 1979 had advised planning authorities to negotiate on a basis so as to avoid appeals. In July 1980 the Minister for Local Government and Environmental Services the Rt. Hon. Tom King said publicly that 'a far less cautious and restrictive attitude should be taken by local authorities' in relation to such requests for planning consent. In the meantime the Company asked several other senior members of the Court to use their contacts within the Corporation of London to see if a change of heart could be effected. Amended plans which sought to meet some of the requirements of the Smithfield District Plan were resubmitted. In May 1981 these revised plans were recommended by the Planning and Communication to the Court of Common Council for approval, where there was some opposition to the proposals. Before it could go before Common Council, the planning application was called in June 1980 for inspection by the Minister for the Environment, Michael Heseltine. After some consideration a decision was taken by the Minister not to intervene. Planning consent was formally granted by the Common Council on 17 September 1981 for building a Hall and offices, but with a requirement that the new development must include some provision for the retention of 'light industrial' premises, in keeping with the spirit of the Smithfield District Plan.

The planning requirement for 'light industrial' provision led to a dramatic breakdown in agreements with the developer. At a very late stage in negotiations, Imry's representatives backed out of the deal as arranged, stating that as a result of the planning restrictions they could only proceed if the Company's equity share of the rental income from the offices was reduced from 25 to 15 per cent. This effectively wrecked the deal. There was understandable consternation on the Company's part. Herbert Graves gave himself 'time to cool off' before he could comment 'within conventional business phraseology' on Imry's withdrawal from the deal.

After this debâcle the Company then undertook negotiations with other potential collaborators and developers. Preliminary discussions took place with the Worshipful Company of Butchers about a joint venture though these apparently came to nothing. In March 1982 the Company undertook detailed discussions with the Heron Corporation, whose chairman and founder was the property developer Gerald

Ronson, later to become embroiled in the Guinness affair. A preliminary agreement with Heron looked very positive for the Company. The Farmers were to enter into a building agreement with Heron, followed by a grant to Heron of a 999-year lease. In return Heron was to construct a Hall and offices and grant an underlease of a shell basement for the Hall plus access at a fixed peppercorn rent. In addition Heron was to pay graduated ground rent, beginning at £5,000 for two years rising to £22,750 per year or 15 per cent of the first £150,000 of rack rents and 20 per cent of the excess, whichever was the higher. On paper this gave the Company an even better arrangement than the Imry deal, with five-year rent reviews as a hedge against inflation and the possibility to rebuild in 150 years. Herbert Graves expressed enthusiasm for the deal and noted that the Heron Corporation was said to have been 'motivated to an unusual extent by the claims of "charitable" foundations and the like, as opposed to those institutions motivated solely by commercial considerations'.

Negotiations with the Heron Corporation progressed almost to completion. Herbert Graves and his colleagues engaged in a marathon series of meetings with Heron's representatives in spring and early summer 1982. But at about 10 a.m. on 13 July 1982, less than 24 hours before what was to be a routine meeting to iron out some remaining legal obstacles, Wilson phoned Herbert Graves with some devastating news. Wilson had just that morning received a letter, delayed in the post, which effectively terminated the agreement, citing a 'change in the market'. In fact Heron's new financial advisers, Rothschilds, had advised the Company to withdraw from several development schemes, fearing that the Heron Corporation, which had earlier grown into one of Britain's largest private companies, was becoming over-extended. The Farmers could take some small consolation in knowing that the pull out by Heron was, in the words of Herbert Graves, 'nothing personal'.

The Clerk, Ian Williamson, writing privately to Herbert Graves, commented 'this is indeed a heavy blow' which would 'place a very large question mark over the whole transaction'. These setbacks caused the members of the Hall Committee to rethink the whole scheme, and the delays which accompanied it caused considerable distress, and some dissent, within the Company about the wisdom of the whole project. Fears were expressed about the strain that the unrealised Hall project was placing on the financial well-being of the Company, especially its Charitable Trust arm in whose name the Hall site had been purchased. Other senior members expressed the view that the Hall project was diverting attention from the Company's support for agricultural education. The Hall Committee deliberated on these problems, while searching for other developers for the remainder of 1982. This delay, which one member of the Court of Assistants referred to as a 'policy of drift', was not helped by the economic recession of the early 1980s. The six different developers the Company approached all backed away from the Company's proposals or were found to be otherwise not appropriate. Members of the Court asked influential friends in the City for assistance but these contacts failed to produce a suitable collaborator for the project. Restrictions in planning consent, by which the floors of offices above the Hall were to be separately let, with adjacent 'light industrial' premises, acted as a disincentive. A surplus of lettable office space and the movement out of the City by some of the larger firms did not help matters. On at least one occasion the possibility of selling the property was contemplated. Despite these difficulties the members of the Committee persisted with their efforts. Charles Wilson provided important advice during this period, consistently recommending that the Company wait out the bad times while maintaining its original goal.

The Farmers and the Fletchers

One line was to resurrect the idea of collaborating with other Livery Companies. The possibility of a joint venture with the Worshipful Company of Fanmakers reached a preliminary phase, but came to nothing. The possibility of sharing Glaziers' Hall also fell through. The Court then considered the possibility of circulating a letter to other Livery Companies without Livery Halls asking whether they would be interested in a collaborative development of the site. As the Court was contemplating this, a fortuitous discussion took place at a lunch at Tallow Chandlers' Hall in October 1983 between Past Master Ronald Borner and Jeremy Garnett, Clerk to the Worshipful Company of Fletchers. The Fletchers, an ancient and venerable Livery Company representing the craft of arrow making for long bows, had been in continuous existence since the late 14th century, their first ordinances being recognised by the City in 1371. The Company, which stands 39th in order of precedence, is one of the few examples of a Livery Company existing by prescription as it has never been incorporated by either Charter or Act of Parliament. As their Clerk explained to Past Master Borner, the Fletchers had once been proud owners of a Livery Hall at the northern end of St Mary Axe. In 1775, however, a fire destroyed the building. The hall was never rebuilt, the site was subsequently occupied as a warehouse and was sold in 1933. Since that time the Fletchers had always wanted to acquire a new Hall. The lunch-time discussion between the two men led to the beginnings of negotiations between the two companies on the possibility of collaboration.

   Both Companies had something that the other lacked. The Farmers had the freehold of a valuable development site. The Fletchers, who lacked the resources for acquiring their own site for a Hall, could provide development expertise. Their Master, Harold Waterman, was a civil engineer with a world-wide practice. The Fletchers' Clerk was a chartered surveyor and a partner in a city firm with long experience in property development. Discussions began in November 1983 at a meeting at the Farmers' Club convened by the Farmers' Company attended by Master Harold Waterman and Clerk Jeremy Garnett for the Fletchers and Past Masters Herbert Graves, Geoffrey Metson and Ronald Borner for the Farmers. From this meeting a proposition emerged that the Farmers would provide the site for the development of a Livery Hall, light industrial premises, office accommodation and a small flat, while the Fletchers would provide a building contractor who was prepared to forgo a developer's profit and take only a building contractor's profit. Negotiations on these lines were protracted, with some hard bargaining by both parties. On 11 June 1984 the Court confirmed a joint arrangement with the Fletchers whereby the Farmers' Company Charitable Fund, which held the property as freeholder, would lease it jointly to the two Livery Companies for 500 years. Ground rents, excluding any rent from the Hall, would be divided 70 per cent to the Farmers and 30 per cent to the Fletchers. The Hall, and the adjoining light industrial area and the flat, were to be managed by a joint committee of the two Livery Companies, its profits or losses to be shared equally.

In September 1984, after the initial meeting with the Fletchers' Company towards the viable completion of the Hall, Past Master Herbert Graves decided to step down as Chairman of the Hall Committee after some 15 years' service. His place was taken by Past Master Geoffrey Metson, who had been acting as Vice Chairman and Honorary Solicitor for several years, and whose law firm of Metson, Cross & Co. had assisted the Company in the legal aspects of the development. Past Master Ronald Borner became Vice Chairman. After this change-over in personnel, negotiations with the Fletchers over the details of the project continued over several months. Leases were prepared in December 1984 and in March 1985 Liveryman John Borner, the son of Past Master Ronald Borner and a chartered surveyor with a wide experience of such projects, joined the Committee. He was later appointed Honorary Surveyor to the Farmers' Company. On 26 November 1985 documents in connection with the development were exchanged. The proposal for development was for the demolition of the existing building on the site and for the erection thereon of a four-storey building providing a Hall in its basement to seat 120, a court room and a reception room, with a kitchen on the ground floor to service the Hall, and on the upper three floors office accommodation, plus a small top-floor flat. Walter Lawrence Project Management was awarded the building contract for around £2 million. The design for the new building was provided by the architects Michael Twigg and Partners. Through the contacts of the Clerk to the Fletchers, Jeremy Garnett, the Scottish Amicable Life Assurance Company were secured as the funding partner for the project.

The legal arrangements were complex. The Farmers' Charitable Fund retained the freehold, but gave a 500-year lease to the Farmers' Company Charitable Fund and the Fletchers' Company. The two Livery Companies then granted a lease of the building for 125 years to the Scottish Amicable which then granted a lease of the Hall, kitchen and top-floor flat to the two Livery Companies at a peppercorn rent. The Farmers' Company Charitable Fund and the Fletchers' Company in turn granted a lease of the same premises to a trading company, incorporated on 6 February 1986 as Farmers Fletchers Hall Ltd. The premises were to be managed by the Joint Hall Management Committee which had been established to supervise the project, the basic membership of the Committee comprising two members and the Junior Warden from both the Farmers' Company and the Fletchers' Company. Past Master Geoffrey Metson was appointed first Chairman of the Committee, with Past Master Ronald Borner and the then Junior Warden, Simon Taylor, as Directors. Each Company was to have the Chairmanship of the Joint Committee for a period of two years. The Farmers' Charitable Fund and the Fletchers' Company were to receive from Scottish Amicable a ground rent calculated as a percentage of the office rents which was eventually settled at 14.35 per cent subject to a minimum of £10,000 per annum, subject to five-yearly upward rent reviews.

Though the last hurdles appeared to have been cleared, there were further delays. The Committee met once a month for more than two years, with many additional meetings. The leases and other documents comprised some 450 pages of closely worded clauses. Extensive legal advice was required to protect the status of the Company's Charitable Fund and learned counsel's direction was sought over this. Further negotiations were necessary to find a firm of caterers to manage the Hall for commercial lettings, as well as making provision for the meetings of both Companies. Further planning permission, this time without public opposition, was sought and was eventually obtained on 26 September 1986. The kitchens, which were to be used by the caterers, fulfilled the provision of a 'light industrial' element requested by the planning authorities. Permission was also granted in the new proposal for letting the offices as a whole rather than to separate firms as earlier required. The work of demolition started on 12 August 1985 and the building work commenced by November that year. By summer 1986 the Joint Committee was able to hold meetings at the site office. Poor weather caused delay. The work was sufficiently advanced to enable the Lord Mayor, Alderman Sir Allan Davis, G.B.E., to lay the foundation on 4 April 1986. Afterwards the Master and Wardens of the two Livery Companies hosted a small reception and lunch at Butchers' Hall attended by the Lord Mayor and the Lady Mayoress and by Alderman and Sheriff Christopher Collett. Fitting out the shell for a Livery Hall involved many detailed meetings with the developers and the architects. Agreements were reached with a firm of caterers for the lay-out and equipment of the kitchens. The Hall had a low ceiling and necessitated specialist advice on acoustics. Because of the position of the motor room for the lift it proved impossible to install special disabled access. The matter was looked into again after

44 The Dining Hall.

the Hall was completed but the Company was advised that it was impossible to provide disabled access equipment without violating building codes.

The long search for a home for the Company in the City, the aim of the Company for over 20 years, culminated in spring 1987. The last task was the completion of the Hall for use. The developer was only responsible for providing the offices and Hall in 'shell form' without funding its fitting and furnishing. It was estimated that the cost of fitting out the Hall would be some £150,000 to each Company. Preparations for outfitting the Hall commenced before the building works were completed. In 1986 the Court of the Farmers' Company asked Past Master Robert Harrison to chair an Appeal Committee, assisted by Past Master Trevor Muddiman, who earlier served on the Hall Committee, and Liveryman John Alston. Contributions were made from within the Company as well as a large number of City and agricultural interests. One hundred and eighty-three Liverymen and five Freemen raised approximately £100,000 by means of donations and covenants. Twenty former Wye students also contributed. In addition some 24 different individuals and organisations, including the Milk Marketing Board, I.C.I., The Royal Agricultural Society of England, The Worshipful Company of Carmen' as well as several other commercial farms,

---

' HRH Princess Anne was instrumental in securing this donation.

banks and other firms gave financial support. Several widows of deceased members, including Mrs. Walter Cardy, also graciously donated to the Hall Appeal Fund. The total received, including recoveries of tax on covenants, was some £180,000. The names of all those who contributed to the Hall appeal were later inscribed in a leather-bound book presented by Past Master Simon Taylor. Included as part of the £180,000 were covenants for specific items of furniture. By this means the Hall was furnished with handsome oak tables and chairs which were embellished with plaques recording the names of the donors. Amongst these were the Master's chair, presented by Past Master Trevor Muddiman, and six chairs given in memory of deceased Past Masters. The Appeal also provided for five elaborate ceiling chandeliers of Czechoslovakian glass. Initially the walls of the Hall were decorated with paintings on loan from the City Corporation but, through the efforts of Past Master Andrew Streeter, Chairman of the Hanging Committee of the trading company, paintings, prints and artefacts were obtained from the Livery of the Farmers and Fletchers. After much searching by Past Master Andrew Streeter, though not part of the original Appeal, a George III mahogany bookcase, originally in the Bishop of Hereford's palace, was acquired by the Company in 1993 for the display of silver and plate under the terms of a generous bequest byPast Master Lt. Col. Attfield Brooks.

45 George III mahogany break-front bookcase origin-ally at the Bishop's Palace in Hereford. Purchased through the generous provision made in the will of Past Master Attfield Brooks, O.B.E., T.D., D.L.

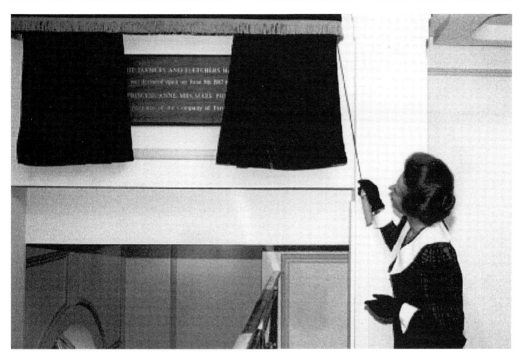

46   The official opening of Farmers' Fletchers' Hall on 9 June 1987 by HRH Princess Anne, Liveryman.

By May 1987 the building work was sufficiently advanced to enable the hall to be let for small functions prior to its official opening. Finally on 9 June, with great excitement amongst both the Farmers and the Fletchers, The Princess Anne, Honorary Liveryman of the Farmers, with the Lord Mayor, Alderman Sir David Rowe-Ham, G.B.E., Master Trevor Kemsley and Antony Taylor, Master of the Fletchers, officially opened the Hall. At long last, after much trial and tergiversation, the first new Livery Company Hall to be constructed in the City of London for more than two centuries was complete. When the Hall was finished it was recognised that it would take time to build up a clientèle for hiring it. The Hall would have to compete for business with the numerous well established Livery Halls. Consequently the Hall was not expected to have an adequate cash flow in its early years and would have difficulty in paying its rent. In 1993 it was decided to appoint a new firm of caterers, Chester Boyd, who were caterers to the Butchers and other Livery Companies. At the same time the Hall was redecorated with a new carpet in deep blue and gold depicting emblems from the crests of the two Companies, a sheaf of corn and an arrow, intertwined. Though the Hall has had some initial financial difficulties both Companies can now look forward to the future with optimism.

Chapter Six

THE COMPANY IN RECENT TIMES

'Once a Liveryman, Always a Liveryman'

The opening of the Farmers and Fletchers' Hall in 1987 marked the culmination of more than two decades of effort to give the Company a permanent home in the Square Mile. At long last the Farmers' Company could claim its rightful place alongside the other older City Livery Companies. During the long struggle to acquire a Hall, undertaken in conjunction with the Company's efforts in running the Wye Courses and helping to set up the Centre for European Agricultural Studies, important changes took place to the internal make-up of the Company. The heavy business of the Company and the Court of Assistants made it desirable to introduce new blood. The Company opened up its ranks to women. New procedures were introduced for encouraging younger members to take up office and for widening participation of the Livery in furthering the work of the Company. At the same time fresh endeavours were made to raise the public profile of the Company in the City of London and new initiatives in education were begun.

During the increasingly busy years of the 1970s and 1980s it became necessary to rethink the organisation of the membership of the Company. The size of the Company grew progressively over the period, but a number of Liverymen asked to be released from their bonds to pay quarterage. In 1973 there were 276 liverymen, 68 freemen, and nine apprentices. In addition there were 15 'yeomen members'—all Australian Young Farmers awarded scholarships under the P. & O. Canberra scheme. The number of liverymen increased by 1980 to almost the limit of 300 allowed by the Court of Aldermen in 1965. Despite this there was also a rise in the number of Liverymen requesting to be released from their bonds. Some 20 men were released in the two years 1981 and 1982, a situation which the September 1982 Court of Assistants described as 'unsatisfactory for a livery company'. There was a perennial difficulty in maintaining links with those members whose livelihoods depended on working far from the metropolis. Emigration abroad, ill health, retirement and long distances from London often meant that it was easy for Liverymen to lose touch with the Company. Requests for resignations were discouraged on the age old principle of 'once a Liveryman, always a Liveryman'.

Periodic surveys were made of the geographical origins of the membership. These revealed that the bulk of the Company lived and worked in the home counties and East Anglia, the latter jocularly dubbed by some the 'Newmarket Mafia'. In order to widen the geographical spread of members, personal approaches were made to suitable candidates coming from less well represented parts of the country. These approaches were in part successful but there was an inherent difficulty. Farming by its nature places demands, so that individuals could only spare a limited amount of time in London and therefore the daily business of the Company tended to be carried on by those closest to the metropolis. The implications of this were spelt out in 1979 when Past Master Herbert Graves carried out a survey which demonstrated that 70 per cent of the members of the Court of Assistants came from just seven per cent of the land area of the whole country.

In the early 1980s various proposals were put forward to strengthen the bonds within the Company while opening up the ranks to new members. Consideration was given in July 1980 to applying to the City Corporation for permission to extend the Livery beyond the limit of 300 set down in 1965, but it was felt that this would entail needless time and expense. As a means of encouraging new members, the practice of granting yeoman membership, originally to young Australian farmers under the P. & O. scholarships until these were discontinued in 1973 (see pp.33-4), was revived by the Company in 1986. This allowed all those members after at least 15 years' membership, to be transferred to yeoman membership on account of infirmity, retirement or other good reasons. This opened up places on the Livery to a new generation, while enabling many of the early members who had retired to retain a connection with the Company.

'Ladies in the City'

Perhaps the most momentous change to have occurred to the membership of the Company in these years was the decision taken in June 1978, two years after HRH The Princess Royal was granted honorary membership, to admit women to the Freedom and Livery. Women had always taken a major role, as wives, daughters and independent proprietors, in the running of Britain's farms but they had been absent from the ranks of the City Livery Companies. Many of the medieval guilds had been open to members of either sex though women were excluded from taking a full part in the public life of the City. The exclusively male atmosphere of the Square Mile has been progressively broken down in the 20th century by the quiet social revolution which has seen women enter all walks of public life.

The right of women to take up membership was raised early in the Company's history. In September 1948 a request for particulars of membership was received from a Mrs. Helen Gordon Dean. The General Purposes Committee considered the matter and recommended that membership of the Company should be limited to men and this position was accepted by the full Court of Assistants. No further applications from women were received and no discussion of the issue took place for more than twenty years. In November 1971 the Master, Frank Garner, wrote to the General Purposes Committee of the Company advising that 'the question had been raised as to whether the constitution of the Company shall be changed so that ladies who are farming might become members of the livery'. At the same time the Clerk had sought out the advice of the Clerk of the Chamberlain's Court of the City Corporation and had been told that women had always been admissible to the Freedom of the Livery Companies, though until 1923 married women had been specifically barred. The Clerk of the Chamberlain's Court further informed the Company that nearly all the other Livery Companies admitted women to the Freedom and that there was nothing to prevent the Farmers from so doing, but that only a few admitted women to the Livery. The General Purposes Committee, after discussing the matter 'at some length', passed the issue to the next full meeting of the Court of Assistants which met in March 1972. That Court took the decision to bar women from entering the Company though it left the door open to future entry when it stated that 'it was appreciated that this decision might have to be reviewed in years to come' and that the Court still had the power, in 'very special cases', to grant Honorary Freedom to women.

There matters rested for several years. In the meantime the doors of other City institutions were gradually being opened to women. The Stationers' Company had appointed a woman to its Court of Assistants as early as 1969. Several other senior Companies, the Common Council and Court of Aldermen of the City of London had opened their ranks to women. In September 1976 the Common Council resolved that 'It would accord with the spirit of the times if Ladies were elected by any Company deciding to do so'. In June 1976 HRH Princess Anne was admitted as an Honorary Liveryman of the Company. The issue of women's entry to the Company was raised the next year when the Court of Assistants considered a memorandum on the subject drawn up by Past Masters Herbert Graves and Frank Garner. It was decided to appoint an *ad hoc* committee to investigate the Company's position consisting of Past Masters Graves and Garner, the Senior Warden, Michael Cheveley, the Junior Warden, Arnold Hitchcock, Assistants Robert Harrison, Alderman Michael Hinton and Derek Pearce. They presented a full report, entitled 'Ladies in the City', in August 1977 which stated unequivocally that there were no constitutional grounds for debarring women from entry into the Freedom and Livery. Their report surveyed the position of other companies and found that the overwhelming majority admitted women to the Freedom, and though a smaller proportion admitted women to the

47 The Master, John Cossins, investing HRH Princess Royal as Junior Warden on 4 October 1999 at the Harvest Service at St Bartholomew's Church. *Left to right*: HRH; the Senior Warden, Richard Brooks; the Clerk, Margaret Winter; the Master.

Livery of their respective companies, the situation was fast changing. Lady Mary Donaldson had become an Alderman and was in line to become Lord Mayor. HRH Princess Anne was on the verge of being elected as Master of the Farriers' Company. In all some 12 Companies, including two of the 'Great Twelve' Companies, had opened up their Liveries to women. It was against this background that the *ad hoc* committee decisively recommended that the Company receive 'suitable applications from women, with no bar, whether formal or informal, to later election to the Court by the usual procedure'. The full Court of Assistants deliberated on the report in December 1977 and it was decided, *nem. con.*, that women were to be admitted to the Livery 'exactly the same way as male applicants'. Shortly thereafter applications were received from two women, but it was decided to defer consideration of their applications pending notification of the whole of the Company's Livery. There was a certain degree of resistance to the admission of women and one male candidate for the Livery was 'blackballed' due to a misunderstanding over Christian names. The strong denunciation of discrimination on grounds of race, gender or religion by Past Master Herbert Graves made at a Court meeting during this period must have done much to persuade others. During summer 1978 a special meeting of the Court, chaired by Arnold Hitchcock, Senior Warden in the absence of the Master, was held at the offices of the Royal Agricultural Society, Belgrave Square, to review the situation and the Court's earlier decision to admit women was reaffirmed. In September 1978 three women, Mrs. Ann Wheatley-Hubbard, Lady Robson of Kiddington and Miss

Elizabeth Creak, were admitted to the Freedom of the Company. In June 1979 Mrs. Wheatley-Hubbard was clothed with the Livery of the Company and in 1985 elected to the Court of Assistants; in 1993 she became the 41st Master of the Company. An independent farmer since the age of 19 and the proud owner of the oldest registered herd of Tamworth pigs in England, Mrs. Wheatley Hubbard's career epitomised the contribution of women to modern British agriculture. Though some outsiders expressed surprise that the Farmers of all companies should have a female Master the Company was delighted that she held such high office. Since the decision to admit women was taken several members have apprenticed their daughters to the Company.

Livery Liaison

During these years further steps were taken to enhance the participation of ordinary members in the Company's affairs. It proved difficult to keep the near 300 members of the Company fully informed of the Company's activities. A Livery Liaison Committee was formed in 1986 to keep members abreast of the latest developments. Suggestions were made to hold social events in those parts of the country where Liverymen lived rather than to confine them to London. The first in a series of Livery Outings was held in 1986 when the Master, Derek Pearce, arranged for a visit of over a hundred Liverymen and their spouses to Goodwood House. This event included a tour of a local Sussex farm and a visit to the evening races. Subsequent outings have been made to Chatsworth House, Hatfield House, Arundel Castle, Glyndebourne Opera and Lord Rayleigh's Farms and Dairy, at Terling, Essex, the latter the home ground of Past Master Sir Nigel Strutt and the then Master Adrian Tritton. That same year saw also the institution of an annual prize of the 'Livery Award' of a silver salver, donated by Past Master Derek Pearce, to be given to that Liveryman outside the Court of Assistants who, in the opinion of the Livery Liaison Committee, made the greatest contribution to the promotion of the Company in that year. The award was to be retained by the recipient for one year and is presented by guests of honour at the Company's annual Livery Dinner. The first award was made to Liveryman and Honorary Surveyor John Borner for his work on the Hall project. Another new initiative of Derek Pearce's year as Master was the creation of a bi-annual newsletter to be sent to all Liverymen to keep the membership fully informed of the Company's activities (see p.94). In 1988 on the recommendation of the Livery Liaison Committee the ceremonial installation of the new Master and Wardens took place before the Livery before the September Luncheon. In 1993 it was decided to move the installation of the Master to immediately after the annual Harvest Thanksgiving service in the church of St Bartholomew the Great, the new Master receiving the blessing at the altar by his chaplain.

48   A basket of fruit and vegetables presented by the Master Elect Richard Brooks to the Rector of St Bartholomew the Great, the Rev. Dr. Martin Dudley, at the Harvest Festival Service, 2 October 2000, with the Master Elect's chaplain, the Rev. Canon Stephen Gregory, in attendance.

Courts of Assistants: New members for Old

During these busy years it became evident that new blood was needed in the Court of Assistants. A generation of younger men joined the Court in the 1970s and 1980s to help shoulder the burden of the increasing volume of Company business. The growing responsibilities of the Court of Assistants necessitated the nomination of new members. In 1972 a Committee was formed to fill vacancies on the Court of Assistants. The Committee recommended that there was 'great merit in the Court encouraging and giving every support possible to those who would make the greatest contribution to the advancement of the Company'. This was to be achieved by approaching members of the Livery who could help the Company. In June 1973 John Cumber, Sir Charles Graham, Alderman Michael Hinton and the Honorary Solicitor, Geoffrey Metson, were elected to the Court. Further new recruits were elected to the Court in the next 10 years. They were mostly active farmers in their 40s and 50s and did much to revitalise the activities of the Court. This group included Trevor Muddiman, who combined farming 1,000 acres in Hampshire, Essex and the Isle of Wight with Chairmanship of the grain merchants Grainec (UK) Ltd. and

Chairmanship of the Hertfordshire and Middlesex branch of the Country Landowners Association; Trevor Kemsley, who farmed cereals and pedigree beef on 950 acres near Maidstone and was active in local government as well as the Sussex Cattle Society and the Smithfield Club; Derek Pearce, Past Chairman of the Farmers' Club, founder of the Farm Management Association, member of the East Anglian Economic Planning Council and Non Executive Director of Frederick Hiam Ltd., Cambridge, which was then an 8,000-acre farm, who had been very active in setting up the Wye courses, and Keith Roberts, a member of the National Farmers Union Council and Chairman of the Meat and Livestock Commission, who farmed 900 acres and managed a further 450 acres in Suffolk. From the late 1960s onwards several sons of Past Masters also joined the Court, including Michael Cheveley (who had acted as Administrator of the Wye courses from their inception until 1990 and who became the first son of a Past Master to take up the office), Arnold Hitchcock, John Borner, and Richard Brooks. By the early 1990s there were several multi-generational families as members of the Company.

The composition of the Court of Assistants as set down in the Company's Charter was stipulated as consisting of the Master, the Senior and Junior Wardens and no less than 20 and no more than 24 Assistants. By the early 1980s it became necessary to rethink the constitution of the Court to make more room for younger members. All Past Masters remained as full members of the Court for their lifetime and, by 1982, 15 out of the 24 members of the Court were Past Masters. As there were no regular retirements from the Court there were no regular vacancies and as the number of Past Masters grew, so the number of Assistants available for possible election as Junior Warden, Senior Warden and Master diminished. In June 1982 the question of making further elections to the Court of Assistants was discussed. The Master, Alderman Michael Hinton, said that he had consulted the Chamberlain's Court and had been told that it was 'quite in order' for the Farmers' Company to provide for Honorary Assistants to the Court who would be able to attend all meetings but who would not be able to vote. The Clerk told the Court that the creation of honorary members of the Court would not require amending the ordinances. A proposal by Past Master Lord Lonsdale to alter the ordinances to increase the maximum size of the Court was rejected as too complicated and, after detailed discussion, it was agreed that five or so years after a Master's year of office such Past Master would then automatically become an Honorary Member of the Court. Though this was agreed in principle the matter was passed back to the Management Committee (later the Master's Committee) for a firm resolution. The Management Committee reported back to the full Court in September, recommending the earlier proposal as well as recommending that all four senior Past Masters (Peter Taylor, Geoffrey Parsons, Stephen Cheveley and Lord Swaythling) should be asked to become Honorary Members of the Court. Though various points of view were put forward by the Past Masters concerned, the recommendation was ultimately agreed. In December of that year all of those requested sent in letters of resignation, with the exception of Lord Swaythling, who preferred to remain a full member of the Court. The Court accepted Lord Swaythling's request to retain his right to vote and added a promise that he would never again be requested to resign. At the same meeting three new members, Henry Nevile, Reginald Older and Andrew Streeter, all joined the Court. Two years later the issue of new blood was raised again and a general appeal to the Livery to nominate 'younger candidates' was made. The resignation of Past Masters as full voting members of the Court of Assistants led to regular elections of new members throughout the 1980s; in all some 10 new members joined the Court after the creation of the system whereby Past Masters after a number of years became Honorary Assistants of the Court. Active recruitment of new members helped to bring on to the Court some notable personalities. This group included Sir Henry Plumb, MEP and Past President of the National Farmers Union, Sir Richard Butler, an Essex farmer who was President of the National Farmers Union 1979-86, Christopher Pertwee, President of the UK Agricultural Supply Trades Association (UKASTA), and Adrian Tritton, Managing Director of Lord Rayleigh's Farms and the famous Strutt and Parker Farms, both located at Terling.

Though this new method of recruitment onto the Court worked for several years, by the early 1990s it was realised that it could take up to 16 years before a new Assistant on the Court might be elected Junior Warden and thus younger Liverymen were being deterred from taking higher office in the Company. Discussions took place with the City Corporation on the question whether the Company's ordinances might be amended to allow for the adjustment in the number of voting members, but this was found not to be possible. Accordingly it was decided in September 1994 to vary the number of Past Masters with full voting rights on the Court. This has meant that new arrivals on the Court have had to wait no longer than eight or nine years on the Court before being elected to the post of Junior Warden. In addition two new posts were created: Senior Past Master, elected annually, and Deputy Master, who is always a Past Master and who deputises in case of the Master's absence at outside functions.

During these years links with the Corporation of London were forged by the elevation of Company members to posts in the City and through the grant of Honorary Livery to prominent members of the City Corporation. Two of the Company's Assistant Clerks have ascended to high office in the City: Alderman Michael Hinton, a chartered accountant who joined the Company in 1960 and acted as Assistant Clerk to his father-in-law Oliver Gordon Sunderland, was elected as Alderman for

Billingsgate ward in 1973. Alderman Hinton, who was then 36, was the youngest member of the Aldermanic bench. On his elevation he expressed great pleasure that he would be 'the first member of the Court of Alderman to be described as "Citizen and Farmer"'. Alderman Hinton gave up his post as Assistant Clerk when he was elected to the Aldermanic bench in 1973 and subsequently went on to become Aldermanic Sheriff in 1977. His place was taken by a member of the Carmen's Company, Christopher Leaver, who was in turn elected as Alderman for Dowgate ward, forcing him also to give up his post with the Company. He expressed his regrets to the Company for leaving after such a short time but quipped, 'there must be something about the office of Assistant Clerk to the Farmers' Company and I recommend that the next appointment signs an undertaking not to go on to the Court of Aldermen'. Alderman Leaver was elected an Honorary Liveryman in 1980 on his election as Aldermanic Sheriff and, in turn, after his election as Lord Mayor in 1981, he honoured the Company by attending the annual Livery Dinner.

49   Badge of Aldermanic Sheriff Michael Hinton, 1977-8, Liveryman of the Worshipful Company of Farmers. Nine-Carat Sheriff of London Badge. The centre being the coat of arms of Michael Hinton Esq. Radiating from the centre in red gold are spokes of a wheel depicting his connection with the Worshipful Company of Wheelwrights. The outer rim of the wheel has seven circular discs applied, engraved with his connections as follows, in clockwise order from the top: 1. Billingsgate Ward Club. 2. Ardingly College, Sussex. 3. Worshipful Company of Wheelwrights. 4. Honourable Society Round Table. 5. The Company of Watermen and Lightermen. 6. The Worshipful Company of Farmers. 7. The City Livery Club.

The links were enhanced as the Company had for a number of years awarded a prize of books to the value of £50, called the Farmers Prize for Attitude and Endeavour, to a boy at the City of London Freemen's School at Ashtead in Surrey. In 1999 the Company decided to award a similar prize to a girl.

The school was founded in London in 1856 for the Education of orphan children of Freemen and moved to Ashtead in 1926. At present the school has some 770 boys and girls.

It is interesting that the first prize given by the Company was awarded to Hugh Broom, who obtained a place on the death of his father. He is now a farm manager and recently attended the Company's Rural Leadership Course at

50 Formal Grant of Livery embodied in Letters Patent under the mayoralty seal (see p. 17, illustration 3).

Seale Hayne.

Thus by the mid-1980s the Company was coming of age. In 1986 the 30th anniversary of the grant of the Charter by HM Elizabeth II was marked by a meeting of the full Court of Assistants at Goodwood House. That year for the first time the Company took part in the Lord Mayor's Show. Plans to participate in the annual pageant had been put forward two years previously. Trevor Muddiman, Master 1984-5, was always determined that the Company should take part in the proceedings. In 1984 he and his Junior Warden, Trevor Kemsley and their wives watched the show from reserved seats on the Embankment. They were sufficiently impressed and determined to mount an exhibit in 1986. The entry fee of £1,500 was raised from personal donations from Court members. As the Company's funds were fully stretched at the time to cover the costs of the Hall, due to open the following year, no help could be expected from corporate funds. However, the Senior Warden, Trevor Kemsley, requested a lorry from Alan Firmin, a well-known Kent farmer with a national haulage business. This most generous gift was donated with the sole proviso that the Kent hops would be displayed on the float. A group of Wye College students volunteered to decorate the float and to stage the exhibit. The students were given a 'float' at a local Kent warehouse to cover the cost of the purchase of materials. The students themselves successfully negotiated with John Deere Ltd. for the use of a tractor to surmount the 'World Harvest Field' which was to decorate the float. The results were splendid. The show took place on a bright Saturday morning in November. Foreign students studying at Wye, representing some 18 different countries, accompanied the Farmers' float in their respective national dress. The exhibit received favourable comments on television and elsewhere. Observers were struck that such a relatively new Livery Company could compete with the industrial, banking and advertising giants which exhibited floats in the show. The only complaint heard was from the Professor of Agriculture at a Wye Governors' meeting to the effect that all his students appeared to be doing was decorating the Farmers' float.

New Initiatives

The years after the completion of the Hall have also seen the Company involved in various new initiatives to broaden the scope of its activities and enhance its core aims. After the 40th anniversary of the Wye Courses it became necessary to rethink the funding and syllabus of the scheme. The cost of running the courses had escalated from £14,000 in 1989 to £32,000 in 1991. It became necessary to adopt the principle, advocated by Past Master Derek Pearce, that all those who could pay their way should do so, with the Company providing bursaries in cases of hardship. Despite this the Wye Courses flourished and went on to a stronger financial footing. New ideas for the Wye syllabus, including support for a Case Study, were put in train. The Company's Charitable Fund received a donation of £5,000 from the Suffolk Agricultural Association in 1993 to be placed in an endowment fund to be known as the 'Suffolk Endowment Fund'. Accrued interest from the fund was designated to further candidates from the county on the Wye Courses. In October 1999 the Oxford Farming Conference, an independent forum set up in 1946 bringing together all the strands of the agricultural and food industries, offered free conference places to candidates of the Company's Wye Course.

The connection with Wye was strengthened in other ways. In 1993 Past Master Michael Cheveley gave his father's extensive collection of antiquarian books on agriculture, ranging from the 16th to the early 20th centuries, to the College. That year the Governors of Wye decided to build a new library and lecturing centre at the College, to be named the Kempe Centre, after the medieval founder of Wye College, Cardinal John Kempe. The Farmers' Company donated £5,000 towards the cost of building a secure room for displaying and storing important collections, of which Past Master Stephen Cheveley's books formed the core. This was named the Worshipful Company of Farmers' Room. The new Kempe Centre was opened by HRH The Princess Royal in April 1997. Later donations of books were graciously made by Past Master Michael Cheveley's widow, Judy.

In the early 1990s the Company experimented with new educational initiatives.

Past Master Derek Pearce mooted the idea of setting up an agricultural education research foundation which would grant research scholarships and bursaries. A pilot project was set up to provide one-off scholarships in 1992. A second year BSc student at the School of Development Studies, University of East Anglia was funded to study perceptions of sustainability of current farming systems in East Anglia. Since then the Company has provided several bursaries and scholarships to individuals; in 1994 Mr. Nigel Poole, a tutor at Wye College, was funded to undertake a study of Spanish agriculture. In addition to these 'one-off' grants the Education Committee also discussed the idea of setting up an another agricultural management course in addition to those run at Wye College. Talks took place with several leaders in the industry and in agricultural education including representatives from Wye College, the Royal Agricultural College, Cirencester, Harper Adams Agricultural College, the University of Newcastle, several Scottish agricultural colleges and the University of Plymouth Faculty of Agriculture, Food and Land Use, which was based at Seale Hayne. It was in the course of discussion between the Chairman of the Company's Education Committee, Philip Gibbons, Assistant Richard Brooks and Martyn Warren (Head of the Department of Land Use Management) and Richard Soffe (a senior lecturer) of the University of Plymouth that the concept of a rural leadership course began to take shape. In August 1995 the Company decided to collaborate with the University in setting up a 12-day course on 'The Challenge of Rural Leadership' to be held every November at Seale Hayne. The purpose of the Seale Hayne course was to provide up-to-date skills to people with at least 10 years' experience in agriculture and who intended to go on to senior positions in the industry. Applicants could also come from those in relevant related industries such as suppliers, land agents and surveyors. The course aims to provide modern expertise as well as to encourage those who take part to fulfil their role in the rural communities as well as in industry. To date, the four courses have taken place with over fifty participants. It is thought to be the only course at the present time devoted to Agricultural and Rural Leadership in Britain, although there are several in the Commonwealth. The most recent initiative by the Company began in September 2000 when an annual prize to 12 agricultural colleges in the country, for agricultural academic excellence from one of their students, was initiated. The colleges have welcomed this new initiative at a time when the number of students wanting to study agriculture has been dropping steadily.

Support for overseas exchanges and apprenticeship, the other two areas where the Company had been active in earlier years, were given new impetus during this period. In December 1988 the Company was told of the £22,000 bequest made to Company by the late Past Master Attfield Brooks. Of this gift some £10,000 was bequeathed to the decoration of the Hall. His personal wish, made known by his sons John and Richard, was that the remaining gift of £12,000 should be invested and the accrued interest should be used to provide aid to Company apprentices, who in the words of Richard Brooks, were the Company's 'seed corn'. The Attfield Brooks Apprenticeship Fund was duly set up in 1989 to assist Company apprentices to undertake overseas travel to widen their education in agriculture, to pursue a formal qualification in agriculture and to help out in the event of unforeseen hardship. In addition it was agreed that some of the fund should be used to pay for bibles, previously paid out of corporate funds, to be presented to apprentices at the commencement of their term of service. A further sum of £11,500 was donated to the Company in 1992 out of the estate of Mrs. Rhoda Brooks. A portion of this was used to make alterations to the display cabinet but the bulk was added to the Apprenticeship Fund.

Another gift helped to renew antipodean connections. In 1991 the then Lord Mayor, Sir Peter Gadsden, chaired the Duke of Edinburgh's British Australian Bicentennial Appeal Trust, which raised money in the UK to fund the gift of a sail-training ship for Australia. At the end of the appeal the Trust had a small surplus to distribute. As a result of an approach made by the Chairman of the Henman Committee, Richard Brooks, the Trustees agreed in 1992 to make a donation of a capital sum of £5,000 to the Company for a scholarship for farming students to gain experience in Australia for up to 12 months. The grant was administered by the Henman Travelling Bursary Fund. By the early 1990s the Company, by means of the Henman grants and the other travelling bursaries, was helping to send more than 20 young farmers a year on work study trips around the world to Australia, New Zealand, the USA, Canada, as well as to India, China, Peru, Argentina, Romania, Kenya and Zimbabwe.

The Company's support for agricultural education in its broadest sense was enhanced by new projects that were designed to help bring town and countryside into closer contact. A new venture came in the form of support for the Surrey Docks Farm. This city farm, situated on 2.5 acres on the site of an old dock yard on the south bank of the river Thames at Rotherhithe, was established in 1975 by Hilary Peters as a place where families and school children from the inner city could come into first-hand contact with agriculture. This was one of the first of a number of inner-city farms designed to bring an appreciation of farming to urban communities. The Company became involved in 1992 when it arranged the donation of two Gloucester Old Spots from the Rare Breeds Trust, courtesy of Assistants Sir Richard Cooper and John Lea, plus a pig ark donated by Liveryman Robert Bowden and six months' supply of feed from Assistant Lea's Company, Morning Foods Ltd. The next year the Company helped to support a poultry festival held at the Farm and the Company has since then helped the Farm with financial assistance and in kind with gifts of animals, equipment and advice. The Company organises visits to the Farm

1 Classroom and cafe; 2 Bee Hives; 3 Chicken houses and animal shelter; 4 Grazing paddock; 5 Pig sties and loose boxes; 6 Dairy and workroom for people with learning difficulties; 7 Compost Heaps; 8 Orchard with 15 different varieties of trees; 9 Area for rabbits and small children; 10 Herb and dye garden; 11 Blacksmith's workshops; 12 Vegetable garden; 13 Duck pond; 14 Greenhouse; 15 Mongolian tents; 16 Wind generator—demonstrating electricity production and providing most of the lighting power.

51   Surrey Docks Farm, alongside the River Thames.

for people from the world of agriculture, commerce and education to encourage support for city farms. Summer 1996 saw the Company take part in schemes to take schoolchildren from the city on visits to working farms. Liveryman Jeremy Courtney welcomed a class of nine-year-olds from Redriff School, Rotherhithe, sponsored by the South of England Agricultural Society as part of the Farmers' Adopt a School scheme, to his East Sussex dairy farm. Past Master Michael Foreman helped to organise a coach visit for 49 children and parents to the Kent County Show, organised by the Kent Agricultural Society. That same summer the Company began to support the National Farmers Education Scheme by sponsoring school visits to farms. Most recently the Company has undertaken to sponsor a series of coach trips for children

52   The Company's stand at the Guildhall Livery Exhibition visited by the Master of the Woolmen's Company and Liveryman of the Farmers' Company, HRH The Princess Royal. *Left to right*: The Master, Mrs. Ann Wheatley-Hubbard; the Senior Warden, Michael Foreman; The Junior Warden, John Borner and the Clerk, Margaret Winter.

from London's schools as a way of promoting a better understanding of the importance of agriculture. The City Farm project and the sponsored farm visits are the most recent examples of the way in which the Farmers' Company has sought a wider understanding of the place of agriculture in the modern world.

Another most generous gift of 3,500 shares in the Shell Trading and Transport Company plc, worth aproximately £20,000, was made to the General Funds of the Charitable Fund in 2001 by Past Master Robin Upton.

Publicity

The Company has also most recently attempted to raise its public profile by means of publicising its activities to the wider world. In July 1994 the Company took part, along with 92 other Livery Companies, in a public exhibition at the Guildhall, organised by the Corporation of London under the auspices of the Lord Mayor, Alderman Paul Newall. The exhibition highlighted the modern activities of the companies and the support given to education, training and charity. In 1996 a historical resumé of the Company, in pamphlet form, was produced for visitors to the Hall and for all public events in which the Company took part. The Company's newsletter, provided for all Liverymen, gradually expanded in format and has become a smartly produced 'in house' magazine under the editorship of Liveryman Kerr Kirkwood (appointed in 1991), with glossy colour photographs, interviews with members, small adverts and reports of the various activities of the Company. Kerr Kirkwood retired in 2000 to be succeeded by Steven Bullock. In 1992 Past Master Trevor Kemsley agreed to act as Honorary Archivist to the Company. The earliest records of the Company were microfilmed. In 1997 Past Master Michael Foreman undertook to obtain photographs of all previous Past Masters back to 1947. The results of his efforts were compiled in a volume to be kept in the display cabinet in the hall, a page being turned at every Court meeting.

The Company was thus becoming more self-conscious of its own by now 50-year history as well as of the continuing need to promote its identity in the City and the wider world. To this end publicity was given to its activities and events. One event deserves special mention, if only because of its unusual nature. In November 1995 the Hall was the scene for a 'Beaujolais Breakfast', sponsored by the Company's caterers, Chester Boyd. For the occasion the contents of Past Master Andrew Streeter's farming museum was transported from Hertfordshire to London for the day. Antique tractors stood outside the Hall and ferried guests around the City. The guests were welcomed by the Beadle dressed as a gamekeeper, attended by Past Master Streeter's dogs. The Hall itself was decked with bales of hay and straw and other old farming artefacts. Some 200 corporate and city livery company guests attended. Alderman Roger Cork (Lord Mayor Elect) was heard to say 'it was the finest farmyard ever seen in the City'. The event was a great success in promoting the public image of the Company in the City. It was with this aim in mind that the Company decided in 1998 to take the thoroughly modern step of appointing a public relations consultant, Liveryman Miss Rosemary Carne of York.

As the century ended the Company could look back with a certain amount of pride at its achievements. After the early uncertain years it had successfully won a place in the august ranks of the City companies. Its membership rolls included some of the most illustrious names in post-war agriculture. At great effort it had succeeded in establishing a highly successful series of ventures in agricultural education and training. It had helped to forge bonds with the agriculturists of Europe, the Commonwealth and the wider world. After many years of planning and through the generosity of its members it had succeeded in building its own Hall. Above all it had achieved what its founders had originally aimed at when they met in the aftermath of the Second World War: to perpetuate the spirit of co-operation in which the importance of farming in the life of the City of London and the nation as a whole could be given a voice.

Chapter Seven

FIFTY YEARS ON:
HOPES AND PROSPECTS FOR THE FUTURE

Though fifty years is a relatively short span of time for a City Livery Company, a half-century mark is an obvious point at which to look back and take stock of what has been achieved and to assess what the future holds. The past is only an imperfect guide to the future and prognostications for any institution for the next ten years, let alone the next fifty years, are to a certain extent bound to prove false. This will be the case with any institution connected to agriculture and the City where continuous change has long been the order of the day. Nevertheless it is important to record for posterity what members of the Farmers' Livery saw as the Company's most significant achievements and aspirations at the half-century mark in its history.

The Company's achievements may seem obvious enough but it is worth recalling what had been done. In the face of some not inconsiderable opposition the original members of the Red Cross Agricultural Fund succeeded giving the spirit of wartime cooperation a permanent embodiment as a City livery company. This new livery company succeeded during the 1950s in building up a wide membership, drawn from all sectors of agriculture and its related professions, including some of its most eminent names. By 1965, as has been seen, the new Company had proved so popular that it was necessary to seek new powers to allow an increase in the number of liverymen. The core of this membership, over 70 per cent, has been and continues to be practising farmers. The remainder of their fellow members are engaged in so-called ancillary activities such as land agents and agricultural valuers, suppliers of seed, animal feed, fertiliser and farm equipment. Thus, while most of the older more established Livery Companies have lost connections with the original trades around which they were founded, the Farmers' Company has retained its roots in agriculture.

All this has taken place against a background of immense change in the countryside. The wartime quest for self-sufficiency in farming was followed by a massive increase in the productivity of British farms. Agriculture has benefited from direct subsidies from the United Kingdom and later the Common Agricultural Policy of the European Economic Community and the European Union. At the same time, the past half-century has seen the steady decline of many small independent farms, a shrinking workforce and the rise of intensive farming and agri-business. This has meant that the bulk of farm production has become, along with processing, marketing and retailing represented by the big supermarket chains, concentrated in fewer and fewer hands. The globalisation of food production and the liberalisation of world commodity markets have turned farming into an international industry dominated by multinational companies, in which the degree of control by national governments and smaller producers has become limited.

More recently a series of structural problems—the fall in commodity prices and the high value of sterling against the Euro—and the fiasco of the outbreak of BSE among Britain's cattle and its links with New Variant CJD have led to a full-blown crisis in British agriculture the likes of which have not been seen since the 1930s. The most recent report by the accountants Deloitte and Touche has shown that average farm incomes have fallen by 90 per cent in the past five years. In many parts of the British countryside a profound shift is taking place way in the way in which people live and work. As the trend towards the concentration of agriculture in larger units continues apace, it is increasingly the service sectors, especially tourism and related activities, which are overtaking farming as the most important sources of work and income in the countryside. As food production becomes increasingly concentrated in fewer and fewer large farm businesses, increasing numbers of Britain's farmers are having to diversify to meet these new challenges or to leave the industry entirely. The younger generation, with wider horizons provided by increased access to higher education and mindful of the financial pressures and sheer toil of farming, no longer automatically follow family tradition and take over family farms. All of this has, and will continue to have, a profound impact on recruitment to any organisation linked to agriculture.

Following the crisis of BSE, the 2001 disastrous outbreak of foot and mouth disease in cattle, sheep and pigs has had repercussions far beyond the agricultural industry and will only aggravate the difficulties experienced by many farmers and may well increase further the move away from farming.[*]

Thus a key area for the future will be membership. As with any organisation, the strength of a livery company must lie in the quality of its members. There has been and will continue to be a need to recruit from the best and brightest in the world of agriculture. Such individuals are hard pressed to devote their time to what is an

---

[*] To help alleviate the suffering of farmers, the Company donated an initial £9,000 to be divided between the Royal Agricultural Benevolent Institution, the Rural Stress Information Network and the Arthur Rank Centre Addington Fund.

entirely voluntary body centred on the City of London. Two questions for the future appear to be how actively should the Farmers' Company seek to recruit new members and how selective should it be in doing so? In a fast changing and ever more demanding business environment it may prove difficult to recruit the most active men and women in agriculture, those in the 30 to 50 age bracket. Because of this the affairs of the Company tend to be in the hands of its more senior members and there is always a need for new blood. This is a dilemma all city livery companies face: how to combine the wisdom of years with the dynamism of youth. There is also the problem of geographical concentration of members from the Home Counties and East Anglia. To an extent this is inevitable but it may be overcome. Information technology, specifically the Internet, may be one way in which a dispersed rural-based membership may maintain contacts with one another. Proposals are being considered which should increase the number of freemen and, as the livery nears its limit of 300 Liverymen, this should mean more competition to join the livery. In time it is hoped that this will mean a younger, more active and dynamic membership.

Agricultural education has been and will continue to be the most important area for the Company's philanthropic efforts. The achievements of founding the courses at Wye College and Seale Hayne, and the establishment of the Centre for European Agricultural Studies, the travelling bursaries and help for apprentices speak for themselves. Nearly a thousand students have attended the Wye Course alone and many have gone on to become leaders in the industry. What is remarkable about these courses is that they were not merely additions to existing educational provision but wholly new efforts that were designed to break new ground, employing the latest techniques in business education and professional training. Thus the Company has acted as a catalyst for change. With British agriculture in crisis, how should the Farmers' Company pursue its original stated aims? Should the Company concentrate its educational efforts on those fortunate few who will weather the coming storms in the industry and emerge as farming's future leaders, or should it help those farmers who may have to diversify into non-agricultural activities? Should the Company specifically set a programme to assist in technology transfer and skills retraining to meet future challenges? How far should the Farmers' educational efforts react to the new challenges of sustainability and stewardship of the countryside and the new environmental concerns for animal welfare and biodiversity? One of the original aims of the Company was, as in its 1948 statement of objectives, 'to bring about maximum production'—a concern understandable enough in the era of wartime blockades and post-war austerity but perhaps not in keeping with modern attitudes towards sustainability in agriculture. Should the educational efforts of the Farmers' Company reflect the changing attitudes to the environment? Future projects may include running a third course along the lines of the present Wye and Seale Hayne courses, sponsorship of annual lectures, support for scholarships and chairs in agriculture at an existing university department of agriculture, or for the setting up of a prestige agricultural leadership course along the lines of those run by the Institute of Directors, in conjunction with an existing business management school, such as the Institute of Farm Management. Perhaps there might be scope for opening up dialogue with the other younger livery companies, such as the Marketors, the Information Technologists and Environmental Cleaners, whose members are involved in industries related to agriculture, processing and marketing, to see if collaborative efforts in education could be made. Conversely, the Company could seek to forge a combined strategy in education with those older established Livery Companies, including the Butchers, Poulterers, Fruiterers and Gardeners, whose original trades were closely linked to agriculture.

An important element in the future will be the no less important work of supporting efforts to encourage greater awareness of farming among the wider public, especially schoolchildren, through city farms and farm visits. As there are some 64 city farms, 14 in Greater London, of which the Company supports one, there is ample scope for expansion if the will and resources are available. Support might also be given to encouraging a greater awareness of agriculture and the countryside in the national curriculum through support for organisations such as the Food and Farming Educational Service. This vital bridging of the gap between town and countryside is entirely in keeping with a City livery company devoted to farming; one of the earliest stated aims of the Company was to 'help to promote a better understanding of the place of farming in the economic life of the nation'. The current difficulties of the industry can in part be attributed to a lack of mutual understanding between town and countryside, abetted by the mixed messages of politicians and the media. The current agricultural recession necessarily puts limits on what can be achieved but, as with other recessions, this one will not last indefinitely. Whatever the outcome of its existing efforts, if the Company is to retain its important role it will have to broaden its support for agricultural education.

The Company is the proud co-owner with the Worshipful Company of Fletchers of a Hall. In roughly a century the building lease of those parts of the site presently leased to other parties will revert to the Farmers' and Fletchers' Companies. More accommodation might then become available on that site and additional income will be at hand for the Company's charitable fund. The area around the Hall is changing rapidly from being dominated by the meat trade to being a fashionable city fringe area popular with office workers and tourists. The redevelopment of Docklands far to the east has shifted the functions of the City outside the Square Mile, and the long-term future of the Smithfield area is uncertain. One thing *is* certain: the hard

53   In 1946, to commemorate the raising of nine million pounds by the Red Cross Agricultural Fund, nine Red Oaks were planted in Windsor Great Park by the order of King George VI to form a cross. In May 2000, during the Livery outing to Windsor, the Master, John Cossins, replaced the one oak that had not survived (see illustration 1).

work, business skills and acumen which members of both companies put into the project virtually guarantee that the options for the future of the Hall look bright.

If the foregoing account of the Company's hopes and aspirations appears complacent, perhaps the penultimate words should go to the late Past Master Stephen Cheveley, who did so much to establish the Company's reputation as an innovator in the field of agricultural education. Interviewed by Past Master Derek Pearce at his home in Kent in 1984 he reflected on the history of the Company and his role in it, offering his own trenchant comments on its future prospects. Asked if he was proud of the Company he responded: 'No, not really. They had better pull their socks up and do something better. They've done jolly well, but the moment they are content they can all go home. The Company of Farmers has no future unless it is doing creative thinking and effort, to help things. There is an unlimited amount of work to be done. If they are self satisfied and sit back, sack them all.' Though it may sound harsh, this is not unsound advice for any organisation.

Perhaps it is best to end a history of so relatively young an organisation with an invitation to future members of the Company. What will the history of the Company be in fifty or a hundred years' time? How best will future liverymen capitalise on the achievements of the first fifty years of the Company's history, building up its membership, finances, educational programmes, hall facilities and links with the City?

The future of the Company will be determined by what happens in the countryside. How will agriculture change in the new century and how will the Farmers' Company have to adapt to meet the challenges to come? Agriculture will inevitably alter in a number of different ways. The half-century since the Company's foundation has seen the application of individual sciences to farming. The future will probably see the increasing application of new emerging domains of science, including biochemistry, pharmacology and computer technology. It is likely that new specialist crops will emerge, brought to the fore by the growing Life Sciences, including crops grown for energy and other industrial uses. Farming will perhaps become but one part of a complex web of industrial and commercial activities involving production, processing, distribution and retailing. Public concerns over the application of science to agriculture could also encourage different trends. An increasingly sophisticated and sceptical consumer-oriented marketplace may encourage the expansion of specialist small-scale production of value-added food relying on traditional methods, including organic farming. Britain's agriculture is on the verge of a new era, not without risks and opportunities. If the Company is to continue to play a constructive role, as it has in the past fifty years, then it will have to respond to these changes.

Likewise, what will become of the City of London and its Livery Companies? How will technological, commercial and political change affect the habits, working practices and traditions of the Square Mile? If the past fifty years in the City is anything to go by, dramatic change will be inevitable. Computer technology is rapidly, transforming the office place. Large firms have decentralised with much of their staff working away from the City, while retaining a core staff and 'front office' in the Square Mile. Though the City of London has largely benefited from the globalisation of financial services the future remains uncertain as other cities, including Frankfurt, pose a potential test to London's dominant role. In this respect the future will no doubt pose challenges and opportunities to the livery companies. Though it is difficult to speculate what this will mean in terms of individual livery companies, it behoves any organisation with a public role to be alive to these trends. Above all, it is worth posing the question to the present and future members: what is the Worshipful Company of Farmers *for*? The progress that has been made in the past fifty years would have delighted the original founders of the Farmers' Company. The foundations for further expansion of the Company's original aims and objects have been firmly laid. If there is no way of knowing what the future holds, there can be some satisfaction from knowing what has been achieved in the past.

Appendix

Court 2001/2002

H.R.H. The Princess Royal, K.G., K.T., G.C.V.O.	Master
C.T. Redman	Senior Warden
P.H. Gibbons, J.P., D.L.	Junior Warden
R.A. Brooks	Immediate Past Master
J.H. Cossins, C.B.E., D.L.	Past Master
C.F. Pertwee, D.L.	Past Master
The Hon. Sir Richard Butler, D.L.	Past Master
W.M. Cornish	Past Master
J.S. Borner	Past Master
M.C. Foreman	Past Master
Mrs. E.R. Wheatley-Hubbard, O.B.E.	Past Master
R.J. Upton, J.P., D.L.	Past Master
The Rt. Hon. The Lord Plumb, D.L.	
Sir Graham Wilkinson Bt.	
N.J. Fiske	
R.R.C. Bloomfield, C.B.E.	
J.A. Naish	
K.H. Johnson	
T.A. Copas	
C.B. Montgomery	
M.E.S. Dart	
J.D. Courtney	
R.A. Bevan	

Honorary Assistants

N.R. Whitwell, J.P.	Past Master
R.S. Borner, O.B.E., V.R.D.	Past Master (Senior)
The Rt. Hon. the Earl of Lonsdale	Past Master
Sir Nigel Strutt, T.D., D.L.	Past Master
A.Q. Hitchcock, C.B.E.	Past Master
R.J. Harrison, J.P.	Past Master
M.H. Hinton, J.P.	Past Master
D.G. Pearce	Past Master
T.W. Kemsley, J.P.	Past Master
S.F.B. Taylor	Past Master
R.M. Older, C.B.E., D.L.	Past Master
A.C. Streeter, D.L.	Past Master (Deputy Master)

Clerk

Miss Margaret Winter

Office-holders of the Company 1952

The Master
1946   Sir Richard W. Haddon, C.B.E.

The Senior Warden
1946   Victor H. Parker, Esq., M.B.E.

The Junior Warden
1946   W.J. Cumber, C.B.E.

The Trustees
1946   The Rt. Hon. Lord Courthope, P.C., M.C., T.D., D.L., J.P.
1946   Sir Richard W. Haddon, C.B.E.
1946   Victor H. Parker, Esq., M.B.E.
1946   Sir Cleveland Fyfe, C.B.E.

The Clerk
1948   O. Gordon Sunderland, Esq., F.C.A., C.C.

The Assistant Clerk
1948   A. Grahame Sunderland, Esq., F.C.A., J.P.

The Court of Assistants
Richard Bolton, Esq.
Stephen W. Cheveley, Esq., O.B.E.
The Rt. Hon. Lord Courthope, P.C., M.C., T.D., D.L., J.P. (Master 1946-53)
The Rev. Cyril L. Cresswell, C.V.O., M.A., F.S.A.
The Rt. Hon. Lord Cromwell, D.S.O., M.C., D.L., J.P.
Major Charles Cullimore, J.P.
William J. Cumber, Esq., C.B.E.
The Rt. Hon. Lord Digby, D.S.O., M.C., T.D.
Sir Cleveland Fyfe, C.B.E.
George N. Gould, Esq., M.R.C.V.S.
Sir Patrick Gower, K.B.E., C.B., C.V.O.
Sir Richard Haddon, C.B.E.
F.C. Hawkes, Esq., O.B.E., M.A.
J.K. Knowles, Esq., C.B.E.
F. Nevill Matthews, Esq., M.B.E., F.A.I.
George Cowper Hugh Matthey, Esq.
Thomas Neame, Esq.
G.R.H. Nugent, Esq. M.P., J.P.
Victor H. Parker, Esq., M.B.E.
Ernest Geoffrey Parsons, Esq.
Claude Luther Pendlebury, Esq., M.C., T.D., F.R.I.C.S., F.L.A.S.
Alec D. Robertson, Esq.
The Rt. Hon. Lord Swaythling, O.B.E.
Henry Cole Tinsley, M.B.E.
R.T. Whitton, Esq., O.B.E., F.A.I.

Masters of the Worshipful Company of Farmers

1946-1953	* The Rt. Hon. Lord Courthope, M.C., T.D., D.L.
1953-1954	* Sir Richard W. Haddon, C.B.E.
1954-1955	* V.H. Parker, M.B.E.
1955-1956	* W.J. Cumber, C.B.E.
1956-1957	* Sir Cleveland Fyfe, C.B.E.
1957-1958	* F.N. Matthews, M.B.E., F.A.I.
1958-1959	* Sir Thomas Neame, V.M.H.
1959-1960	* F.C. Hawkes, C.B.E., M.A.
1960-1961	* The Rt. Hon. Lord Cromwell, D.S.O., M.C., L.L., J.P.
1961-1962	* S.W. Cheveley, O.B.E.
1962-1963	* The Rt. Hon. Lord Swaythling, O.B.E.
1963-1964	* E.G. Parsons, C.V.O., C.B.E.
1964-1965	* H.C. Tinsley, M.B.E.
1965-1966	* P.B. Taylor, T.D., J.P., D.L.
1966-1967	* W.L. Cardy
1967-1968	* E. Hitchcock
1968-1969	* H.C.H. Graves, O.B.E., B.Sc.
1969-1970	N.R. Whitwell, J.P.
1970-1971	* W.M. Balch, F.R.I.C.S.
1971-1972	* F.H. Garner, M.A., M.Sc., F.R.Ag.S.
1972-1973	R.S. Borner, O.B.E., V.R.D., F.C.A., A.C.M.A.
1973-1974	The Rt. Hon. The Earl of Lonsdale
1974-1975	* B.L. Barker, F.R.P.S.I.
1975-1976	* Lt. Col. C.A. Brooks, O.B.E., T.D., D.L.
1976-1977	Sir Nigel Strutt, T.D., D.L., FRASE
1977-1978	* M.C. Cheveley, B.Sc. (Agric), F.R.I.C.S.
1978-1979	A.Q. Hitchcock, C.B.E., M.A.
1979-1980	R.J. Harrison, J.P.
1980-1981	* C.G. Metson, O.B.E.
1981-1982	M.H. Hinton, J.P., F.C.A., F.R.S.A.
1982-1983	* Major Sir Charles Graham Bt.
1983-1984	* K.E. Roberts, O.B.E., J.P.
1984-1985	* C.T. Muddiman
1985-1986	D.G. Pearce, F.R.S.A., F.B.I.M., F.R.Ag.S.
1986-1987	T.W. Kemsley, J.P.
1987-1988	S.F.B. Taylor
1988-1989	R.M. Older, C.B.E., D.L., M.F.H.
1989-1990	A.C. Streeter, D.L.
1990-1991	R.J. Upton, J.P., D.L., M.A.
1991-1992	* Sir Henry Nevile, K.C.V.O.
1992-1993	* A.J. Tritton, B.Sc.
1993-1994	Mrs. E.R. Wheatley-Hubbard, O.B.E.
1994-1995	M.C. Foreman
1995-1996	J.S. Borner, B.Sc., F.R.I.C.S.
1996-1997	W.M. Cornish
1997-1998	The Hon. Sir Richard Butler, D.L.
1998-1999	C.F. Pertwee, D.L.
1999-2000	J.H. Cossins, C.B.E., D.L.
2000-2001	R.A. Brooks

Clerks

1947-1966	*	Oliver Gordon Sunderland, F.C.A. (Deputy)
1966-1975	*	Oliver Gordon Sunderland, T.D., F.C.A., C.C.
1975-1976		The Rev. Dr. A.C. Kirk-Duncan, Ch. St.J., M.A., D. Phil.
1976-1979	*	Stanley G. Jones, F.C.I.S.
1979-1986		Ian G. Williamson
1986-1988		Christopher Maunder-Taylor, F.R.I.C.S.
1988-1993		J. Patrick Jackson, F.C.A.
1993-		Miss Margaret Winter

* Deceased

Deputy Masters

1989-91	Past Master Michael Hinton, J.P.
1991-93	Past Master Trevor Kemsley, J.P.
1993-95	Past Master Arnold Hitchcock, C.B.E.
* 1995-96	Past Master Michael Cheveley
1996-98	Past Master Robert Harrison, J.P.
1998-00	Past Master Simon Taylor
2000-	Past Master Andrew Streeter, D.L.

Honorary Almoners

* 1955-61	Claude Pendlebury, M.C., T.D.
* 1961-73	Past Master Walter Cardy
* 1973-74	Past Master Peter Taylor, T.D., J.P., D.L.
* 1974-76	Past Master William Balch
1976-86	Past Master Ronald Borner, O.B.E., V.R.D.
1986-97	Past Master Robert Harrison, J.P.
1997-99	Past Master Robin Upton, J.P., D.L.

Chairman of the Almoners Committee

1999-	Past Master Robin Upton, J.P., D.L.

Honorary Solicitors

* 1955-66	Lt. Colonel Norman Letts, O.B.E., Liveryman
* 1966-93	Geoffrey Metson, O.B.E., Master 1980-1
1993-00	Richard Woof
2000-	John Thorpe, Liveryman

Honorary Surveyor

1986-	John Borner Master, 1995-6

Honorary Archivists

1993-2000	Trevor Kemsley, J.P., Master 1986-7
2000-	Arnold Hitchcock, C.B.E., Master 1978-9

Honorary Editors of the News Letter

1991-2000	Kerr Kirkwood, Liveryman
2000-	Steven Bullock, Liveryman

Honorary Public Relations Officer

1999-   Miss Rosemary Carne, Liveryman

Livery Salver Award Winners

1986   John Borner
1987   Christopher Pertwee
1988   *No Award*
1989   T.M. Cracknell
1990/93   *No Award*
1994   Kerr Kirkwood
1995   R.W. Kemsley
1996   J.D. Courtney
1997   M.E.S. Dart
1998   D.L. Tinney
1999   *No Award*
2000   R.A. Bevan

Livery Outings

1986   Goodwood House
1987   —
1988   Newmarket and National Horse Racing Museum
1989   Wye College
1990   Chatsworth
1991   Hatfield
1992   Arundel Castle
1993   Lord Rayleigh Farms
1994   Harewood
1995   Thames River and Lambeth Palace
1996   Glyndebourne
1997   —
1998   Wernpole
1999   Woburn (see 1987)
2000   Windsor Castle and the Great Park
2001   Sandringham, cancelled due to Foot and Mouth Disease

Advanced Farm Business Management Courses

Course	1	January	1963	Folkestone
Course	2	January	1964	Folkestone
Course	3	January	1965	Folkestone
Course	4	January	1966	Folkestone
Course	5	January	1967	Folkestone
Course	6	January	1968	Folkestone
Course	7	January	1969	Hexham
Course	8	January	1969	Folkestone
Course	9	November	1969	Folkestone
Course	10	January	1970	Folkestone
Course	11	November	1970	Folkestone
Course	12	January	1971	Folkestone
Course	14	November	1971	Folkestone

Course	15	January	1972	Folkestone
Course	16	November	1972	Folkestone
Course	17	January	1973	Folkestone
Course	18	November	1973	Folkestone
Course	19	January	1974	Folkestone
Course	20	November	1974	Folkestone
Course	21	January	1975	Folkestone
Course	22	November	1975	Wye College
Course	23	January	1976	Wye College
Course	24	November	1976	Wye College
Course	25	January	1977	Wye College
Course	26	November	1977	Wye College
Course	27	January	1978	Wye College
Course	28	November	1979	Wye College
Course	29	January	1979	Wye College
Course	30	January	1980	Wye College
Course	31	January	1981	Wye College
Course	32	January	1982	Wye College
Course	33	January	1983	Wye College
Course	34	January	1984	Wye College
Course	35	January	1985	Wye College
Course	36	January	1986	Wye College
Course	37	January	1987	Wye College
Course	38	January	1988	Wye College
Course	39	January	1989	Wye College
Course	40	January	1990	Wye College
Course	41	January	1991	Wye College
Course	42	January	1992	Wye College
Course	43	January	1993	Wye College
Course	44	January	1994	Wye College
Course	45	January	1995	Wye College
Course	46	January	1996	Wye College
Course	47	January	1997	Wye College
Course	48	January	1998	Wye College
Course	49	January	1999	Wye College
Course	50	January	2000	Wye College
Course	51	January	2001	Wye College

The Challenge of Rural Leadership Courses

Course	1	November	1996	Newton Abbot
Course	2	November	1997	Newton Abbot
Course	3	November	1998	Newton Abbot
Course	4	November	1999	Newton Abbot
Course	5	November	2000	Newton Abbot
Course	6	November	2001	Newton Abbot

INDEX

Note: page references in **bold** are to illustrations, those with suffix 'n' refer to footnotes.